IT'S A VET'S

Alex Duncan – a pseudonym ... a best-selling
author who has been described by the New York
Times as 'one of the really great comedy writers of
England' – first wrote this true story in 1961. It
became a classic, selling more than thirty thousand
copies in its UK hardcover edition. Since then it
has been translated into different languages and
has enjoyed enormous success wherever it has
appeared. The time is long overdue for this
paperback edition which has been only slightly
edited to bring it right up to date.

'Animal in every sense of the word: and it is easily
the most original animal book I have read, and
quite the funniest in years.' *The Countryman*

'The author will have you in stitches.' *Sunday
Pictorial*

IT'S A VET'S LIFE

Alex Duncan

A STAR BOOK
published by
W. H. ALLEN

A Star Book
Published in 1976
A Howard & Wyndham Company
44, Hill Street, London W1X 8LB
Reprinted 1976

Copyright © 1961 by Alex Duncan

Printed in Great Britain by
Richard Clay (The Chaucer Press), Ltd., Bungay, Suffolk

ISBN 0 352 39861 2

AUTHOR'S NOTE

This is the story of a veterinary surgeon, his patients the animals, and the 'owners' the animals own.

There is no reason why real animals should not identify themselves with the animals in this book. But there is every reason why real 'owners' should *not* identify themselves with the 'owners' in this book; they'd certainly be wrong – which would make a cat laugh.

CHAPTER ONE

'If you attend a dog whose mistress calls it *darling* watch out, especially if she calls her husband by his full Christian name. Nine times out of ten the dog will be a hysteric.'

'And the husband?' I asked Uncle Simon.

'Well, Michael, he could be anything from a manic depressive to a fellow with a persecution complex. Remember, the husband should be none of your business, but if you aren't careful he soon will be . . . And that's the only piece of advice I'm giving you.' Uncle Simon locked the cabinet of patients' files and flung the keys on the desk. 'The surgery's all yours.' He looked as pleased with himself as if he'd just tossed the keys into the English Channel.

'Where's your forwarding address?' I asked.

'You won't need one. I've arranged for my guns to be sent to the boat.' Simon picked up an apple-green anorak, the latest Himalaya-Sahara model from Lillywhite's and put it on in front of the mirror.

'I wasn't thinking of your guns,' I told him. 'What if I wanted to consult you about a patient?'

'You won't be able to, Michael, that's all there is to it. I have no idea where I'll be – in India, in Africa, on top of a mountain – in some jungle; but wherever it is I'm not going to travel thousands of miles to pick up letters at the nearest Cook's. Don't look so depressed,' he patted me on the shoulder. 'I suppose you do know as much as any other young vet?'

'Of course I do.'

'Well then, you've nothing to worry about. Besides, you'll have my Mrs Whiting.'

His Mrs Whiting, tightly swaddled in a starched coat with too many jerseys underneath, had marched into the surgery. 'Your taxi's waiting, Mr Morton.' The juvenile face under her iron-grey hair went pink. 'Here's something you'll find handy.' She gave him a silver flask curved to fit a fleshier hip than my uncle's. 'Used to be my father's. The old man always carried it when he went game-hunting – you can still see the dent from the arrow a Baluba tribesman slung at him – well, good luck, Mr Morton.'

'Very kind of you, Mrs Whiting – where are the dogs?'

'Waiting outside.'

They were more than waiting. Prince, Uncle Simon's huge alsatian, was resting his forepaws on the open window of the taxi breathing hard at a scared driver; Ted, the golden spaniel, was flop-flopping between front door and car barking at Prince; Rocco, the black poodle, had sat down beside the open car door, and the Pug was circling round the poodle in case Rocco made a move to get inside.

I expected a noisy demonstration, but Uncle Simon simply told the animals to sit and they sat, side by side on the cobblestones at a safe distance from the car. He patted each head in turn and got in. The driver, with a grunt of relief, pushed back his cap and started the engine.

'See the dogs get enough exercise,' said Uncle Simon.

'I'll take them for good long walks,' promised Mrs Whiting, fervently.

'Good girl.'

It was an astonishingly emotional farewell for them. The taxi swung out of the Mews. Uncle Simon's Tirolean hat disappeared round the corner.

'Good,' said Mrs Whiting. 'Glad he's off at last. He's been having too many colds lately.'

Uncle Simon had always wanted to go on safari but ever since his army days his plans had gone awry. The Veterinary

Corps, instead of sending him to India or Africa had landed him in Aldershot or Catterick. Instead of looking after camels or elephants he'd found himself looking after the colonel's lady's cats or the regimental goat until, bored and liverish, he cut his pension losses and bought an almost extinct practice in a Knightsbridge mews.

For the first time in his life he worked; he worked hard and he soon made so much money that he could not afford to go on safari. I was his last hope. After talking me into becoming a vet he thought I should be grateful enough to run his practice for a few hundred pounds a year. I disagreed.

A qualified vet is entitled to a decent salary as an assistant, and since Uncle Simon had made up his mind he would not pay more than twelve hundred pounds a year I took jobs in the provinces. The advertisements all *sounded* attractive. In Northumberland I was given, as promised, a suite with my own bathroom; but I was out among the cows at all hours, getting stuck in the mud in my chief's derelict pre-war Austin. The bathroom, far from being a luxury, turned out to be essential life-saving equipment.

In Bournemouth the routine of the practice had been responsible for the nervous breakdowns of two of my predecessors; assistants there were employed for the sole purpose of performing one particular operation, sterilising cats. The endless queues of flat-dwelling pussies soon made me scream in my sleep. And Wales had been all abstract art, air-conditioning, and an aesthetic chief prepared to pay up to three thousand pounds a year provided his assistant was willing to don pure silk leisure wear.

It was the leisure wear that aroused Uncle Simon at last. He was appalled; he would not have a nephew of his languish in gaudy silks. Besides he was still hankering after a safari. We got down to some serious bargaining. No, he wasn't offering me more than twelve hundred but something far better, *incentive*. If I ran his practice single-handed for a year he would give me a fifty-fifty partnership *provided* I lost none of the families who had consulted him for two years or more and provided I gained a minimum of six new regularly attending animal-owners.

Meanwhile his bank would pay my salary and I would have the free use of Mrs Whiting's services, his house, his 1924 Rolls Royce Silver Ghost (with four-wheel brakes) and his four dogs. The dogs, he assured me, were a great asset in keeping one fit. A professional man tended to look a fool – or worse, an eccentric – if seen running round the park like a mere student. But to run in the course of training dogs was quite dignified; in fact it was good business for a vet.

I accepted the dog-show as I accepted the whole proposition, not of course without having our agreement signed and sealed by a firm of lawyers.

It was a gamble for me but the odds were reasonable; I could trust myself to keep my uncle's regular patients. Why not? I was good-tempered, fairly patient, and I was fond of animals. The half-dozen new animal-owners, if they did not come of their own accord, I would pick up socially, probably by joining a club. The near-by Royal Ouse Yacht Club was bound to have a large dog-owning membership.

Of course there was the question whether I'd be able to afford joining a good club; Uncle Simon's twelve hundred was already heavily committed. But what was a year of penury if at the end of it my income would go up to six or eight thousand? No, Uncle Simon had not been ungenerous. He was almost certainly saving me from hard labour under a variety of chiefs or from mortgaging my earnings years ahead in buying a partnership or a single-handed practice.

Uncle Simon's house, in its solid mahogany way, was not bad either. It was as reassuringly undistinguished as Mrs Whiting who managed it, who assisted in the surgery, and who had known Simon's regular patients for the past ten years.

I was examining the supply of surgical instruments when Mrs Whiting came in, dressed in a tweed skirt and a brown suède jacket. 'Mr Michael, will you be out for dinner?'

'Why, did my uncle go out on Sunday night?'

'Well, yes. He had beer and steak-pies at the Crown – it's not expensive,' she explained, understandingly. 'But if you'd rather, I'll make you an omelette.'

'No, please don't bother. I'll try the steak-pies.'

'Right. I'm off with the dogs then.'

Without the jersey-stuffed surgery-coat Mrs Whiting was quite shapely I thought, watching her from the window. She had slim, long legs and surprisingly small feet for a country-bred English woman. At forty she was as fresh and wholesome as a young girl, and she might have looked pretty with the help of a good hairdresser. It was an idea; Mrs Whiting needed help. I felt sure she had been in love with Uncle Simon for years. I would teach her how to make him notice her. She had lost her husband when his plane had crashed at the end of the war; I didn't think there had been anyone else, judging by her self-consciously easy stride.

She had fastened the dogs' collars and picked up Pug's lead. Pug immediately took hold of the poodle's lead, Rocco took the spaniel's lead and Ted the alsatian's. Prince obviously was the pace-setter of the cavalcade. Linked together they marched off in single file, entertaining a small girl who was skipping over the cobbles at the far end of the Mews.

When I went out for supper the child was still there, leaning against the lamp-post, watching the entrance to the Mews.

'Where's Mr Morton?' she asked me.

'He's gone on holiday.'

'Have the dogs gone away too?' She sounded anxious.

11

'No, they're staying at home.'

'With you?'

'Yes, my name's Morton too; Michael Morton.'

'I'm Joanna,' she told me, gravely. 'I've got a bird – it's a special one.'

'What kind?'

'A thrush.'

'Yes, that *is* special.'

'My mother doesn't like him singing – *Daddy* gave him to me,' Joanna added, as if it explained everything. Perhaps it did. 'Pippo likes ants' eggs – Daddy buys them in Harrods.'

A light went on above us and the window opened. 'Jo-anna!' shouted a harsh Mediterranean voice.

A blast of Rigoletto made it unnecessary for Joanna to reply.

'Come in at once!' the voice drowned Rigoletto. A heavy face framed in tousled black hair appeared. 'You're not to wait for your father!'

'But Mother!' Joanna's eyes filled with tears. 'I just want to see whether he's got the ants' eggs for Pippo.'

'Your father will have forgotten, as usual,' the voice became shrill, 'and if you don't come in immediately I shall *sell* Pippo.' The window slammed shut and Joanna, with a last glance towards the main road, ran indoors.

I went and looked at the chromium name-plate of these new neighbours of mine. 'Alfred Donizetti,' it said, 'Maker of Society Gloves.' I felt for Alfred Donizetti; Society Gloves plus Mrs Donizetti did not seem a promising combination for a happy life.

A long American car with ferocious eyebrows came sliding round the corner and stopped outside the Donizettis' house. The owner, a stout agile little man, had seen me reading his plate.

'Your daughter's been waiting for you,' I told him. 'And for the ants' eggs.'

12

'Ah, yes,' he smiled, 'I have the ants' eggs here – you live in the Mews? I know, I know,' he beamed, 'you have bought Number Seven. At last they have sold Number Seven. In winter our house is very cold with the empty Number Seven beside us.'

'No, I'm sorry, I haven't bought the house next door. I'm Mr Morton's nephew. I've taken over his surgery.'

'So he is gone – pity about the Number Seven. Mr Morton gone – it will be good against his colds, *non e vero*?'

'Could you tell me the way to the Crown?' I asked.

'Sure. Out the Mews, turn right, then come the traffic-lights, and you take second street on the left.' His head bent closer and he glanced at the lighted windows of his house. 'Is good evening at the Crown – you see Miss Claremont.'

I could not help seeing Miss Claremont. She was draped over a stool at the bar, dressed in lilac-coloured shaggy trousers and an engulfing shaggy jersey; her blonde hair hung to her shoulders straight and smooth and she wore a smooth lilac-pointed siamese cat round her neck. The two young men standing over her wore rugged twenty-guinea sweaters (buy what is devil-may-care or just very, very suave) in clerical grey and lovat respectively. The three of them were drinking Coca-Cola.

I'd seen many pictures of the Hon. Claire Brown-Claremont. The Sunday papers had 'covered' her ever since she was elected the prettiest debutante of the last bunch presented to the Queen. If she went to a first night it was 'news'; if her parents went to spend the winter on a Greek ship-owner's yacht in the South of France the gossip-columns rumoured quarrels in the family and Claire's marriage-plans – naturally of a kind her parents would detest. Claire's lilac cats too were a talking-point; she dressed in colours that either matched her cats' coats or in toning shades.

'Oh, Claire!' A third young man burst into the bar, also

13

dressed in a rugged twenty-guinea sweater. 'I've been looking for you all over the town.'

'Hello Winky,' said Claire, unmoved by his excitement.

'Tell me Claire, are you still working for Tiger?'

'Of course; I've been with him for *two* months.'

'Oh, good. You see, I've got a problem on my hands.
Mama's had a horrible idea – she wants to give a birthday
party for my twenty-second.'

'Ridiculous,' Claire sympathised.

'Absolutely awful,' grey-sweater agreed. 'Have a coke,
Winky.'

'Yes, thanks, I need it. Look Claire, will you help? You
know Mama, once she's got an idea in her head there's
nothing one can do – but it wouldn't be so bad if *we* made it
a *real* party. What do you think?'

'Too bad it's almost winter,' said Claire. 'We could have
used your patio for a South American Katanga.'

'A Katanga?'

'Winky, aren't you with it? A Katanga's the sort of party
where no one knows what's going to happen next. I suppose
we could make it a South Pole thing – you know, tents,
camp-fires and that sort of thing.'

'The patio'd be too small. Couldn't we do something
indoors?'

'Well – Tiger's got some lovely Chinese furniture in the
shop just now. Perhaps he'd lend it to us.'

'We'd need mandarin-coats,' suggested lovat-sweater.
'Uncle Dick might lend us his – he lived in China.' He
looked at his watch. 'He'll be at the Royal Ouse now – shall
I go over and ask him?'

'Yes do, John,' said Claire.

The Royal Ouse Yacht Club clearly was the club for me.
To become a member I'd need a proposer and a seconder.
I looked at Claire's lilac cat, and the cat looked at my steak-
pie. I softly scratched my plate; the cat softly descended

Claire's shoulder and slid along the bar. No one seemed to have noticed. I gave the cat my only piece of steak; it stared at me with cool blue eyes and asked for more in a loud baby-cry.

Claire turned, noticing me for the first time. 'Chou-en-Lai!' she called. 'What are you doing! Come here!' Chou-en-Lai arched her back and rubbed herself against my shoulder. 'How extraordinary! She doesn't normally like strangers.'

'Siamese are very sensitive,' I said, 'she knows I understand cats.'

'Have you got siamese?'

'Well, no, but I'm a vet.'

'Oh!' Claire, Winky and grey-sweater turned my way. 'Do you think Chou-en-Lai looks well?' asked Claire. The cat gave another look at my pie, decided there was no meat left, and lazily remounted Claire's shoulder. 'You see,' Claire gave a proud smile, 'she knows we're talking about her – but she's been odd the past few days; since she's been staying with Mummy in the country she's been awfully quiet.'

'Has she been with other cats?'

'No!' A stricken look came into Claire's violet eyes. 'You *don't* think! Mummy *has* got a tabby – a boy. Oh Chou! What has that ghastly Mouser done to you?'

'He may not have done anything,' I suggested.

'Could you tell? – I mean, so soon.'

'How soon is it?'

'Well, Chou's been in Hazelbridge five or six weeks.'

'Then I should be able to tell, possibly even without laboratory tests.'

'I simply *must* know – will you look after Chou-en-Lai for me? You see we lost our vet – he was an Irishman – he drank creme de menthe, and last week he drove into a tree – and now we haven't even got anyone to look after Aunt Jane's horses.'

15

I said I'd be delighted to look after the Brown-Claremont ménage, and I meant it. Here undoubtedly was my first group of patients and I was confident they would be regular patients. I was bound to last longer than an Irishman who got tight on creme de menthe. I pencilled my name on one of Uncle Simon's cards; Claire wrote down her address on the back of an old theatre ticket. It was a Mayfair address.

'Michael, you *will* come tomorrow, won't you?'

I promised I'd call about lunchtime, after my morning surgery.

John returned, reported that his Uncle Dick was willing to lend his mandarin-coats for Winky's party, and was told that Claire had found a vet.

'That's a bit of luck,' he said, giving me a welcoming nod. 'You *know* Uncle Dick's hound, Claire – he's rather a problem. Have a coke everyone.'

I swallowed mine, trying for the umpteenth time to discover a flavour – any recognisable flavour.

'Don't you like Coca-Cola?' asked Claire. 'You don't drink creme de menthe, do you? I think there's some left –'

'No thanks.' I put down my case. 'I'll have a coke after I've examined Chou.'

'What do you think of my flat?' asked Claire. She looked as nervous as if *she* had been awaiting an examination for pregnancy. She wanted to put off the unhappy moment.

'Very original,' I said.

'Do you know, everyone says the same.'

I was not surprised. Two walls of her lounge were painted pale lilac, the colour of her cats, two walls were striped lilac and mustard yellow, and the ceiling was black with grey smears that looked as if someone had walked on it. Suspended from the ceiling by invisible threads hung five perfect paper-replicas of pheasants which floated about disconcertingly whenever Claire or I moved. There were sundry arm-

16

chairs covered in pale lilac velvet – oddly enough standing on the floor, or rather on a dark lilac carpet – a white bookshelf surmounted by a reproduction of Picasso's 'The Kiss', a white desk and an organ-sized white record player.

Claire seemed to be waiting for a more specific comment. 'Did you employ a firm of interior decorators?' I asked.

'No, it was my own idea – very lucky too. Tiger – you know, St George Clemens – came in the day after it was finished. He offered me a job on the spot. He's got the most marvellous antique shop in Chelsea; I suppose you know it –'

I told Claire I didn't. I told her I hadn't lived in London except as a veterinary student. Since then my friends had dispersed. Claire looked the most exciting girl I'd ever seen in a pair of tight, shaggy pants; I told her, sadly, I didn't know a soul in London.

'Oh Michael, how deadly!' she exclaimed. 'You must come to Winky's party – are you sure you won't have a Coca-Cola?'

'No, thanks – perhaps I'd better –'

'Yes, of course – well, you've met Chou-en-Lai,' she said, lamely. The little cat on her shoulder half opened its eyes, and subsided again. 'And this,' Claire scooped another siamese out of a satin-quilted easter-egg on her record-player, 'this is Mao-tse-Tung.'

'They're both beautiful cats,' I told her, genuinely impressed. 'But why call she-cats male names?'

'I didn't know any other important oriental ones – besides, Chou and Mao *sounds* feminine, doesn't it?'

'China's leaders wouldn't agree, but I think you're right.'

Claire solemnly plucked Chou from her shoulder and handed her to me. 'I'll go next door while you examine her – will it hurt?'

'No, of course not. Don't worry.'

Claire retreated to the door. 'Perhaps I *should* have had

17

Chou operated on, like Mao. But you see, with Chou I hated the idea – she's rather more feminine than Mao; I thought – well, it does spoil their sex life, doesn't it?'

Palpating Chou's abdomen I thought the little lilac cat must have enjoyed sex life in the country; she was full of kittens. Unless Claire intended entering her in a show I could see no harm in her bearing the kittens; they were unlikely to spoil the figure of this two-year-old mother.

Chou regarded the examination as a new kind of game. She did not complain, and when I had finished she rolled over on her back giving me to understand that she liked being scratched under the chin. Though Chou was an aristocrat of a cat I did not think she would be a problem patient. If there was a problem it would be, as with most thoroughbreds, the owner.

I called Claire, and she came in at once with a tray of Coca-Cola bottles and glasses. 'Is she – ?'

'Yes,' I said, trying not to sound unimpressed – or worse – indifferent. 'But I think having kittens will be good for her.' I thought I'd appeal to Claire's feelings about a happy sex life. 'It wouldn't be normal at her age not to have them.'

'But she didn't have a proper mate,' said Claire, miserably.

'*You* don't think so, but I'm sure Chou doesn't mind in the least. Actually I think a cross between siamese and tabby is a most attractive combination.'

'Well,' said Claire, doubtfully, 'I suppose you are right – though it isn't really proper.'

'If you approve of a good sex life –'

'I certainly do.' Claire sounded defiant. It suddenly occurred to me that she was a puritan down to the last inch of her shaggy pants. That would also explain the Coca-Cola. It would explain the Coca-Cola drinking young men in twenty-guinea sweaters. But it did not explain her firm round little breasts with nipples that showed even through the shaggy mohair of her jersey. She was no more than twenty,

18

of course . . . yet when I was a student girls of twenty had not been the least puritanical. I wondered whether a revolution had taken place among the young in the past five years or so. Odd, I was twenty-eight, yet people like Claire or Winky or John seemed to me to belong to another era. Had the sputniks so scared them that they were taking refuge in traditional, puritanical 'clean-living' and establishing a new tradition of safe alcohol-free Coca-Cola?

'You think I'm being silly about Chou and Mao,' said Claire.

'It's difficult not to be silly about beautiful animals.' I decided on a guess. 'They're your first siamese, aren't they?'

'They are. Perhaps that's why I'm behaving as if *I* were having kittens.' She looked almost happy. 'Is there anything special I should do for Chou?'

'She's perfectly healthy, but I'll let you have some powdered vitamins to keep her in condition. Mix them with her food.'

I promised to visit Chou regularly until her confinement, and Claire was seeing me out when John came up the stairs accompanied by a red-bearded, freckled character in a rust-coloured sheepskin coat.

'Tiger!' exclaimed Claire. 'How sweet of you to come. John dear! Michael, you *can't* go now! Let's have some lunch. I've got some frozen things in the fridge.'

'All right.' Tiger had a surprisingly deep, rumbling voice. 'But *I* am going to do the cooking, Claire. How's the patient?'

Claire reported in the kitchen, while Tiger made a meal of frozen chops, peas and chips, and we talked cats over coffee in her bottle-green and blonde dining-room.

Back in the lilac lounge Tiger promised to take one of the kittens, and I managed to bring the conversation round to John's Uncle Dick, his problem dog, and the Royal Ouse Yacht Club.

19

At four o'clock John promised to give his uncle my address. 'If he doesn't want a vet at the moment he'll be needing one pretty soon.'

At five past four I got into the car, with John and Tiger looking on, visibly impressed by the distinction of the Silver Ghost. They stayed impressed even when the Rolls wouldn't start.

'The engine's got cold,' growled Tiger, sympathetically. 'Got a starting handle?'

Between the three of us it took half an hour to resuscitate the Silver Ghost. It sprang to life just in time for me to reach Knightsbridge for my evening surgery. Or so I thought. I had not taken into account its petrol-consumption. In the middle of the traffic, just outside St George's Hospital, the Silver Ghost spluttered and stopped.

'The waiting-room's full,' said Mrs Whiting. 'You're late.'

'I know, I know. I had trouble with the car. How much does it eat?'

'It's not bad – it does about twelve miles per gallon.'

'Not bad, if your income's ten thousand.'

'Better hurry,' advised Mrs Whiting. 'You've got five dogs, a budgie, and three cats waiting.'

'Do any of them pay cash?'

'One or two – *I* keep the books,' she let me know, not unkindly. 'And there were three telephone calls.'

'Anything urgent?'

'You'll have to go after dinner.'

'In the Silver Ghost?'

'It'll be too far for walking.'

There were no desperate cases among the animals; eye-drops for the budgie, bronchitis among the dogs, cats with enteritis or sore throats; mostly ailments that would respond to injections of penicillin or one of the other antibiotics.

It was the last dog, or rather its owner, that took up most

of my time. The dog was a small, very old sand-coloured mongrel, its owner a very old lady in a black coat that was too thin for the frosty weather.

She came into the surgery with the dog on a wooden tray, wrapped in a piece of blanket. 'Please may I see Dr Morton?' she asked Mrs Whiting. 'It's Andy. He's had an accident and – well, you see Dr Morton's always been so kind to Andy.'

'I'm sorry,' Mrs Whiting relieved her of the tray. 'Mr Morton is on holiday. This is Mr Morton's nephew. He is now looking after the animals.' Mrs Whiting gave me a file-card. *Miss Emily Shaw* it said; her address was Archway Road, Highgate; the dog Andy was fifteen years old and had a long history of heart and eye-trouble.

'He's been so good,' said Miss Shaw, taking the chair Mrs Whiting had pulled up beside my desk. 'The bus-conductors didn't like my carrying him like this but he didn't make a sound, so they let us stay.'

'You carried him all the way from Highgate, Miss Shaw?'

'Well, Dr Morton's been so kind; I didn't want him to come out. It's so far.' She watched me unwrap the dog, her face anxious and tense. 'Have I done right, Doctor? You see, Andy can hardly see – he fell downstairs – I thought if he'd broken a leg – I read somewhere you should put injured dogs on a tray –'

'Yes,' I told her, 'you've certainly done the best thing.'

The little mongrel stared at me with blind eyes. The irregular rhythm of its heart, the shivers passing down its flanks told me that it was in considerable pain. Yet its jaws remained stoically clamped together.

Andy's left hind leg was almost certainly broken, but before examining it properly I wanted to relieve the pain. I knew I should put that dog to sleep for good; it had cataract in both eyes, a bad heart and, judging by the unpleasant smell, bad teeth. It was the look on Miss Shaw's

21

face together with the queer silence of the dog that decided me to take no chances; I put a very small amount of novocain in the syringe, enough to take the edge off the pain but not enough to affect the heart.

'I'm afraid Andy's leg *is* broken,' I told Miss Shaw.

'Will he live, Doctor?'

'I can pin the leg, and with careful nursing –'

'I can watch him day and night,' said Miss Shaw, quietly. 'I haven't anyone else to take care of.'

No one to take care of, no one taking care of *her*. How often I had come across the same situation at my other surgeries! A lonely old animal-owner with an old animal that should be put to sleep. But who was to suffer, the owner or the dog? Clearly Andy *had* to be kept alive; it was lucky for him that he had once been a very tough little creature, that even now he was taciturnly willing to put up with life.

'Don't worry, Miss Shaw,' said Mrs Whiting, carrying the tray with the dog behind the operating screen. 'Andy's quite strong.'

I pinned the leg, with Andy keeping still partly from exhaustion partly because the injection had eased the pain, and when I put a light splint on he even raised his head showing interest in the smell of my gloves. There was no way of rewarding Andy for his courage; he couldn't have chewed a lump of sugar, and I had no soft chocolates.

'If you like,' said Mrs Whiting, 'I can give you supper after you've made your calls.'

'I was just thinking of it,' I told her, gratefully.

'But you'll probably be back rather late – you have to see two old patients as well as a new one.'

'Never mind. Don't wait up for me.'

'Rubbish; you must eat. Miss Shaw, I'm going to make a cup of tea. You'll join us, won't you?'

'Oh, please don't trouble.' Miss Shaw went over to Andy and stroked his head. The dog made a feeble attempt at wagging its stumpy tail. 'He's better already, isn't he? Thank you, Doctor, thank you so much. If you'd just tell me what to do for him I'll take him home.'

'Miss Shaw, I'm going to drive you home. That long bus journey wouldn't be good for Andy.'

'No, Doctor, we've given you enough trouble. I – perhaps I could get a taxi.' She touched her handbag, obviously counting in her mind whether she had enough money for the fare.

'It won't be out of my way,' I said, counting in *my* mind the gallons Simon's Silver Ghost would eat between Archway Road and my first call in Hampstead. 'I have to visit a dog practically next door to you.'

Miss Shaw and Andy lived above a health-food shop with a window full of sick-looking cashew nuts in splitting packets and dusty bottles of a half-dozen varieties of vinegar. I carried Andy up the stairs to Miss Shaw's bed-sitting-room with its evil old-dog smell, thought of the Silver Ghost's petrol gauge, and recklessly promised to call every two days or so until the leg had mended.

The dog that lived 'practically next door' belonged to a large well-manicured house in Hampstead, almost a gallon of petrol away.

It belonged to Mrs Topper, who was waiting for me at the open front door. 'So you've come at last,' she said in a small, disagreeable voice.

'I had a busy surgery,' I said, reminding myself that Mrs Topper was one of the regular animal-owners I could not afford to lose.

'My dog might have choked himself to death.' She was not interested in other people's animals. 'In here!'

As we entered the brightly lit lounge there was a thud, followed by a patter of small falling objects. At the same moment I saw a miniature white poodle lying on its back

23

on a persian rug, giving a brilliant imitation of a fit. I might even have accepted that fit if it had not been for the over-turned box and a scatter of candies on the floor.

'Pookie!' exclaimed Mrs Topper. 'Have you been a naughty boy eating things? Oh no, of course not! It was that cat again. Is em's ill, poor darling?' She knelt down beside the poodle. 'Archibald!' she shouted, 'Archibald!'

A tall grey man in a grey city suit came in.

Mrs Topper, from her absurd height of five-foot-nothing, glared at him. 'Archibald, how often do I have to ask you to remove that cat of yours when Pookie is ill! Poor darling – the cat does upset him. The cat's got no business in the house.'

The cat, sitting on the arm of a chair, tucked its tail round its front paws and sardonically watched the poodle's convulsions. The expression on its face infuriated Mrs Topper. 'Archibald – if anything happens to Pookie –'

'Come on, puss.' Mr Topper scooped up the cat. 'Let's go for a walk.'

'Archibald, I may need you – if Pookie has to have medi-cine you might have to –'

'All right, Mary – I won't be far.'

'Well, aren't you going to *do* something?' Mrs Topper turned on me. 'The poor darling's been suffering like this for *hours*.'

'Let's sit down,' I suggested. It seemed to me the poodle was tiring of its contorting efforts. Between spasms it managed to assess me out of the corner of one eye. 'What has he been eating today?' I asked.

'The usual, of course.' Mrs Topper went into a detailed description of the brand of dog-biscuit Pookie favoured, the way Pookie liked his steak prepared, his favourite walks and his favourite trees.

'Could you please bring me some water for him?' I interrupted at last. 'Just drinking water.'

Mrs Topper gave me an I-knew-you-were-a-young-fool look, but she did leave the room.

'Pookie,' I said to the poodle, 'if I had to listen to that nasty little voice all day long *I* would probably roll on the carpet, but' – I picked him up by the scruff – '*you* are going to learn self-control.' By the way Pookie's ears arched up I could tell that he perfectly understood my tone of voice. To emphasise my point I gave him a good wallop where it hurts but doesn't harm. '*Now, sit!*' I put him down, and he sat, ears up, one forepaw raised, indicating an engaging preparedness to obey.

'Pookie, down!' I ordered, as Mrs Topper came in with the water. Pookie flattened himself on the run, his four paws stretched out, head innocently turned up towards his mistress.

'Have you given him something?' asked Mrs Topper.

'Yes – would you let him have the water now.'

'Is he all right?'

'Perfectly.'

'Come to Mummy, darling,' coaxed Mrs Topper. To her obvious surprise Pookie obeyed. 'What *was* the matter with him?'

'Hysteria.'

'I beg your pardon?'

'Nerves.'

'Yes, he's highly strung – still he can't have been *really* ill if he's recovered so quickly; how much are you going to charge me for his – *treatment*?'

'Ten pounds, Mrs Topper.'

'We pay cash, you know.'

'Ten pounds,' I repeated, firmly.

She rummaged in a large grubby Woolworth bag, and brought out some crumpled notes. 'Here you are – a vet's business must be something of a gold-mine. Since you *are* here I want you to look at my sister's cat. It's staying with

25

us, and it hasn't eaten for three days. Come along.'

I might have known Mrs Topper would get something for nothing; but the agreement with Uncle Simon made it impossible for me to object. I was in no position to antagonise one of his 'regular' animal owners.

'I can't understand it,' she said, leading me into a fabulous, gadget-ridden kitchen. She pointed to a marmalade cat lying dejectedly on the draining-board. 'This – thing normally eats at least thirty pence worth a day – so my sister said. *I* know it's greedy, but now, just to be awkward, it's gone on hunger-strike. I suppose *you* will say it's sick.'

The cat did not look at all sick; and when I touched him he purred ecstatically. Cats, more sensible than humans, frequently associate affection with other pleasures of the senses, especially with food. As I had anticipated the marmalade cat suddenly jumped down to the floor and made for his dinner.

He *almost* picked up a piece of meat and then, unexpectedly, sniffed at the plate and retreated backward. I took a closer look at the plate; the congealed gravy round the rim showed plainly that the plate had not been washed for some days. The cat sadly gazed at his food, turned his head, and then stared at Mrs Topper, his wide amber eyes full of contempt. 'You slut' was my interpretation.

'Would you let me have a clean dish, please?'

'A clean dish!' Mrs Topper shrugged her shoulders. 'Oh, well, I suppose you know what you're doing.' She opened a cupboard full of clean dishes, examined about a dozen, and finally – grudgingly – gave me a chipped soup-plate.

I picked up a spoon and put the more appetising parts of the food on the clean dish. '*Now* will you give this to the cat.'

The moment Mrs Topper set down the plate on the floor the cat dived for it. He crouched down, tail excitedly moving from side to side, and just kept his head in the dish, chewing and purring at the same time.

'Extraordinary!'

'No, Mrs Topper, it's not extraordinary. Cats are fastidious creatures. And there are some that dislike eating off dirty plates.'

'I might have known!' Mrs Topper made it sound as if she had known. 'Of course, my sister's a perfect fool with animals – Archibald! Archibald! Show the vet out, will you.' She disappeared up the stairs without a 'thank you' or 'good-bye.'

'You must forgive my wife,' said Mr Topper, coming out of the lounge. 'But, you know, she's a perfect fool with animals.'

'My husband adores wild creatures,' said the elegant wife of Dr Armstrong. 'He'd never have pets as ordinary as dogs or cats.'

We were drinking martinis in a pretty sea-green room above Dr Armstrong's consulting rooms in Harley Street. By the time I had finished with the Topper family Dr Armstrong had been called out to a patient and Mrs Armstrong had succeeded in calming mine. My patient, a full-grown red fox, was lying curled up in his basket fast asleep. The only sign that he was not always so peaceful were marks on the legs of the antique chairs, all of them gnawed to splinters.

'As wild creatures go Renard hasn't been a bad pet,' Mrs Armstrong assured me. 'He chews up wood but at least he doesn't pull down curtains and china like our last lot – they were bear-cubs.'

'What was the trouble with Renard today?' I asked.

'Oh, nothing much. I think he needed a worm-powder – I gave him one after my husband went out. You see, Peter refuses to believe Renard could have anything as undignified as worms. He – I mean the fox – was also biting his tail again. I soon stopped that – *also* after Peter went out. I

27

bathed the tail in tonic water. Renard can't bear anything bitter.'

'It seems to me you don't need a vet, Mrs Armstrong.'

She smiled, showing white, even little teeth. 'I only need a vet when my husband's at home. He won't let me do anything for his pets – he believes in calling in the specialist; well, naturally, being a specialist himself.'

'Dr Armstrong's a psychiatrist, isn't he?'

'Yes, that's why we can't have cats or dogs,' she explained, with amusement. 'The only fit companion for city-man is a splendid wild beast,' she gave a good imitation of a male lecturer, obviously her husband. 'A splendid wild beast to remind its effete owner of the simpler, saner life beyond the concrete jungle. Oh, well, as psychiatrists go Peter's pretty sane. Have some more Martini.'

'No, thanks, I have another call tonight.'

'Pity.' She got up, and followed me to the door. 'You must come again – a social visit, I mean – and tell me about nice ordinary cats and dogs. What are you going to see now?'

'Well, unless my housekeeper misunderstood the phone message I'll be seeing a snake.'

CHAPTER TWO

A giant cobra in Soho? Edging the Silver Ghost through a narrow street of foreign restaurants to its sleezier end I began to have my doubts. For once even Mrs Whiting might have got an address wrong. The Silver Ghost was eating petrol while I trundled in and out of Soho looking for a parking place. When I did find one it was a couple of miles away, in a Bloomsbury square.

I trudged through the chilly sleet, down Tottenham Court Road, past dejected groups of Africans and West Indians in the Charing Cross Road, on into the gaudily lit lane where my cobra was supposed to live. It did not seem a nice place for a cobra; every second window displayed advertisements for 'experienced catering', 'introductions' or 'sympathetic treatment'. Beyond the business-centre was a no-man's-land of dark doorways, which abruptly ended in a blaze of purple neon lights.

The cobra, according to Mrs Whiting's note, lived at the *Purple Pigeon* which advertised itself as THE TOP-MAN'S TOP TO TOE SHOW and THE BEST DRESSED UNDRESS SHOW IN TOWN. There was a large windowful of photographs, all of girls naked apart from the Christmas tinsel that covered the pubic hair, and edifices of ostrich feathers that covered their heads. However, my cobra did live there; it was photographed interlaced with Lakshmi, the *Fabulous Snake-dancer*. And Lakshmi, though she wore Christmas tinsel as well as coiled silver snakes covering the tips of her breasts, did look fabulous. She was small, curvacious, with delicately moulded limbs and she had an enchanting little face; narrow, full-lipped, with large luminous eyes reminiscent of a bush baby.

Her black hair, smoothly brushed into a bun at the nape of her neck, gave her an air of innocence in striking contrast to the surrounding nudes.

'You coming in for the show?' The pugilist in the purple livery, who had been watching me, came so close that I could smell the garlic in his breath.

'No, I want to see Miss Lakshmi,' I said.

'Yeah? Don't they all. Bill! 'E wants to see Miss Lakshmi!' Another purple pugilist appeared. 'Look 'ere, if you wanta see the show, come in – if you don't, beat it.'

'Miss Lakshmi rang up and asked me to see –'

'Yeah?' said number two pugilist. 'I've 'eard that one before. Now be sensible – we don't want no trouble 'ere –'

'You'll be in plenty of trouble if you don't show me in. Miss Lakshmi's snake is sick, isn't it. I'm the veterinary surgeon –'

'Crikey!' Number one pugilist's battered face went to pieces. 'That's right, Bill. Cobby's been poorly all day. Sorry, sir – but there's a lot what try it on, see. Take 'im up, Bill.'

Bill led me through a purple-lit bar into a small scarlet-lit theatre full of men. An invisible pianist was playing 'In a Monastery Garden' while the curtain went up on a sylvan scene of cardboard greenery interspersed with naked girls as wooden and virginal as the trees. The girls didn't stir, neither could I imagine any man *being* stirred by all that chaste and chilly nudity.

'Artistic, ain't it,' said Bill proudly.

We went down a passage littered with theatrical scenery and empty beer-crates and up a shaky wooden staircase to a cabbage-scented landing with four doors.

Bill thumped on the one at the far end. 'The vet's 'ere, ducks. Got yer woollie on?'

'Thanks, Bill.' Miss Lakshmi did have her woollie on, a sexless brown, hand-knitted cardigan which clashed hideously with the scarlet velvet vine-leaves covering her about as adequately as a bikini would have done. Her feet were stuck in a pair of zipped fur-lined boots which did not entirely obscure the fact that she had beautiful legs. 'Come in, Mr Morton.' She opened the door a little wider. 'It's kind of you to come – so late in the evening.' She had the soft educated voice of a Girton girl.

'Not at all, Miss Lakshmi,' I said, rather stupidly.

'My name's Julia Hanley . . . oh Cobby!' The angrily dilated head of a serpent, all of twelve feet long, rose from the floor. Julia squatted down and took the swaying head in her hands. 'There Cobby, there. It'll soon be over – she's had such a bad time of it, Mr Morton.'

It was then I noticed that two-thirds of the snake was gleaming like polished metal while the tail-end was still painfully squirming inside its *old* skin. The shedding skin was lying behind the snake like Cobby's own fragile ghost, brittle, faintly animated whenever the snake's body moved, and oddly pathetic.

'Getting out of the skin's hurting Cobby, isn't it? I don't know why.' Julia was still fondling the snake's head. 'I used to watch cobras in India – *they* didn't have trouble getting rid of the old skin.'

'Snakes that live outdoors have the help of undergrowth and trees,' I said, wondering what substitute I could use.

'Oh dear!' Julia looked depressed. 'Daddy told me it wasn't fair taking Cobby to London. What am I to do now?'

'Only one thing we can do – get her stripped before she knows that's happening. Can you keep a hold on her head?'

'Yes, of course.'

'All right.' I took off my coat, dropped it on the black horse-hair sofa, and took up my position at the tail of the snake. 'Hold tight!' Encircling with the fingers of both hands the cobra's body I gave a quick hard pull that freed her of the old skin in one move. The front of the snake reared,

31

tumbling Julia on the floor, the tail lashed against my shin. A hard kick from a horse wouldn't have hurt as much, but I was more worried about Julia, still in possession of the hissing head.

'Cobby's not poisonous.' Julia sat up. 'Daddy had her fangs removed – anyway, she wouldn't hurt *me*. Look! She's out of pain now.' The snake's head, deflated, had sunk gently against Julia's shoulder, the rest of its body was lying still and relaxed. 'Perhaps it was that lump on her side that made things so hard for her,' said Julia.

The lump was the size of a man's fist. 'What has she eaten?' I asked.

'Well, nothing. She's off her food. She hasn't eaten anything for nine months.'

I explained to Julia carefully, so as not to make her feel she didn't know how to take care of her own snake, that the cobra was constipated. Instead of eating its normal meal every three or four months the constipated snake had lost its appetite, it had become weak and therefore unable to dispose of its old skin at a comfortable speed. Had the cobra not been weak it would probably have broken my leg instead of just bruising it.

We sent Bill to a chemist's for a purgative, and we poured it into the unresisting, exhausted Cobby. I told Julia to feed the snake in the morning; and that should have been the end of my visit. But then Julia, rummaging among the pots of grease-paint on her dressing-table, produced a bottle of whisky. I thought of Mrs Whiting keeping my supper hot, sat down on the horse-hair sofa, and surrendered to Julia's hospitality.

She talked of India. While a north wind was rattling the windows of her shabby dressing-room she talked of the heat and of temples in the hills, of tropical birds and the snakes that had been her childhood pets. Her father had been in the

32

Indian Army and later an official employed by the Indian Government.

'What does he think of your working in a strip-tease joint?'

'He doesn't know what I'm doing – my parents live in Leamington Spa. They think I'm a dancing instructress – in a girls' school.'

'Why aren't you?'

'It's not so easy,' said Julia. 'I did try to find that sort of job, but I have no qualifications – no diplomas. Actually all I can do is Indian dances. Without Cobby I wouldn't have got even this job – though it's not bad.'

'Don't you mind being stared at?' I couldn't bring myself to say 'by a lot of dirty old men', but Julia understood.

'I don't have to strip as much as the other girls; and after all, they're the same men that would stare at me on any beach.'

'Don't they wait for you when the show's over?'

Julia laughed, 'Oh, they wait. But it doesn't get them anywhere. I never go out of here alone – at least not at night. You see, the owner of the *Purple Pigeon* has a van, and after the show Bill drives us home. Mr Malloy's very strict.'

'My Malloy? The owner of a place like this?'

'Why not!' said Julia, hotly. 'Mr Malloy's an elder of the Presbyterian Church and its treasurer.'

An elder and a church-treasurer, owner of a strip-tease joint where the girls stripped to the strains of 'In a Monastery Garden'; I thought it best not to make insinuations about so formidable a character. Besides, Julia was one girl I meant to meet again, with or without her snake.

'What would be Mr Malloy's reaction if *I* called for you after the show?' I asked.

'Oh, I don't think he'd object – you are Cobby's doctor, aren't you?'

This, I decided, was *not* a situation to be handled with tact

33

if I was not to be bogged down by professional etiquette. 'Yes, I'm Cobby's doctor,' I said, 'but I'm also a bachelor of twenty-eight – an *unattached* bachelor with a special interest in snake-dancers.'

'I'm not accustomed to snakes,' I told Mrs Whiting. She had given me my third cup of tea but I still couldn't stop yawning. For once the den beside the kitchen was comfortably warm; even the dogs couldn't be bothered to get out of their baskets. Only Prince sat up, bored but patient, while Joanna was dressing him up in her school hat and scarf.

'I suppose snakes have their troubles,' said Mrs Whiting, 'just like other animals. But you know animals are sensible; *they* don't expect you to keep fussing once you've given them their treatment. It's their owners who are difficult; for your own protection you've got to show them you're a busy man, or they'll take advantage of you – expect you to solve their problems as well as their pets'.'

'Sometimes the problems of pet and owner are interrelated.'

'Prince, keep still,' commanded Joanna. 'Your hat isn't straight – that's better. Now, Pug, you can have a yellow bow.' She pulled a handful of ribbons from her pocket. 'And Rocco's bow is red because he's a black poodle – no, Teddy, you can't have one. Spaniels don't wear bows; you'd look silly. But I have a lump of sugar for you.'

'Joanna, shouldn't you be going?' asked Mrs Whiting. 'You'll be late for school.'

'Oh, all right Auntie Whiting.' Joanna picked up the hat Prince had shaken off and reluctantly jammed it on her head.

'Put your scarf on, it's cold.' Mrs Whiting got up and buttoned the child's coat. 'Off you go, Joey. I'll be taking the dogs out before evening surgery; want to come?'

34

'Yes, *please*.'

'Very well, but don't forget to ask your mother first.'

'No.' Joanna hugged Prince, and ran out.

'Is she a permanent member of the household?'

'Just about.' Mrs Whiting collected the breakfast plates. 'Poor little thing – a cuckoo's a better mother than Mrs Donizetti!'

'How about Joanna's father?'

'Alfred Donizetti's out most of the time, and it's not surprising. No, Joey's got no one apart from her thrush.'

'She's got our dogs, anyway.'

'They aren't *hers* – are you going to visit Miss Shaw's, Andy?'

'I think I'd better – I promised the old lady I'd keep an eye on that leg.'

'Thought you would. Only,' Mrs. Whiting hesitated, 'don't be late again. It's too easy to get into a habit of over-working. Your uncle used to overdo it – tired himself out, and then he kept getting colds.'

'Well, I didn't tire myself out last night. I even had time to think of you.' I put on the table a hairdresser's card Mrs Armstrong had, rather generously, given me. 'The fox I visited last night has a smart mistress; she gave me the address of her hairdresser for you.'

'For me?' Mrs Whiting stared at me as if she expected my face to break out in a rash. 'Why?'

'Because I asked her who her hairdresser was. Because you have nice hair which you treat abominably.'

Mrs Whiting's hand went up to the blue silk scarf on her head which failed to conceal that her hair was twisted into innumerable old-fashioned curlers.

'I'll make you a present of a hairdo at Mrs Armstrong's salon,' I told her, 'a Christmas present.'

'It isn't Christmas.' Mrs Whiting picked up the teapot and made for the kitchen.

I followed her. 'Christmas isn't far off. But that's beside the point. I want you to try this hairdresser, Muriel.' Mrs Whiting looked up but she didn't seem to mind my using her Christian name. 'Muriel – Mrs Armstrong looked very pretty.'

'I dare say; I don't suppose she's grey, fat and forty,' said Muriel, gruff with shyness.

'She's grey and forty, but not fat. Neither are you when you aren't wearing too many jerseys under your surgery coat. In future you won't have to; *we* are going to turn up the central heating.'

'Michael, this is a big house. It's expensive to heat –'

'My uncle can afford it. You've slaved long enough, saving his money.'

'We had to build up the practice almost from scratch. Your uncle wasn't well off –'

'He is now. Well, how about that hairdo?'

'It was kind of you, Michael.' She glanced at the card, not without interest. 'He'll be an expensive hairdresser.'

'Two pounds a time; that's after he has undone your handiwork.'

'Not bad – but it's absolute nonsense, Michael. I'm no chicken and I've always managed –'

'My own hair,' I finished for her.

Muriel turned away, smiling. 'You make me sound like an old –'

'You make yourself sound like – whatever you're thinking of.' I slipped the hairdresser's card into her pocket. 'Is it a deal?'

'Well, all right – provided *you* show some sense; no night-work, snakes or no snakes.'

Cobby, gleaming in her new skin, looked sleek and dangerous twisted about Julia's brown body. Every night for a week I had watched their snake-dance, sitting in the stuffy little theatre among fat old men or frustrated lean ones, watching the snake's every move, always half expecting the nasty crunching of cracking ribs. It was too nerve-racking; I felt grateful when Julia suggested meeting me *after* the show in the coffee-bar round the corner.

It was the sort of place where one gave one's coffee an extra stir in case the waitress's false eye-lashes had dropped in. The customers, sitting on chromium stools padded with doughnuts of sponge-rubber, had a fine view of two Soho streets and of the girls tottering past on tiny heels, their bare knees wobbling, their heads swollen with sheepskin or rabbit busby-hats.

At first it seemed to me the majority of passers-by had the faces of criminals but after my second coffee I recognised that the faces were nothing worse than vacant. They were late-evening city faces, the faces of people who had managed to get through yet another city day into the privacy of their personal dreams.

'My square's a honey,' an adolescent voice sang behind me. He was a pale boy, clinging on to a guitar. 'My square's a haoo-hao-honey –'

'*Mais certainement*,' said the man on the stool beside me. 'Is *sehr* simple.' His grubby well-shaped hands gestured under the nose of a smooth young man in a cheap, super-smart suit. 'I have the drawing at home – is all finished – ready for you,' he wheedled.

'What abaht the safety device?' asked the smooth character, clearly a second-rate profiteer. 'Withaht the safety device I can't promise yer a market.'

'We must make the prototype first – I make the safety-device direct on the model – is simple.'

'No, no, that's no good to me.'

'Look, you miscomprehend – let me explain –' The grubby-handed inventor pleaded. The imposing Goethe-head bent close to the profiteer's. His accent thickened until it became unrecognisable. Perhaps it was French, perhaps Russian – perhaps he'd had to drag his inventing genius through half a dozen countries and as many languages. This, I thought, was London; this was the world where a nice young girl in a scarlet velvet vine-leaf danced with a snake. I loathed the idea. Something would have to be done about that.

'Hello, Michael,' Julia had come up behind me, her luminous grey eyes smiling. 'What were you thinking?'

'I was thinking of you – coffee?'

'No, let's walk.'

'My car's in Soho Square – wouldn't you like me to drive you home?'

'No, I love the town at night.'

It did have its charm; Oxford Street with its million-penny glitter, with its infinite variety of voices, Indian and African, German, Spanish, French, Italian, and sounds mysteriously unrecognisable.

I took Julia's hand and put it in my coat pocket. It felt as warm and dry as her snake. 'How was the show tonight?'

'Full house. Cobby's full of beans – well, beans would give her indigestion again, wouldn't they? I mean, Cobby's fitter than she's been for months – thanks to you. Captain Franks sent up a note saying he'd never seen Cobby perform better.'

'Who's Captain Franks?'

'One of our regular patrons.'

'I thought Mr Malloy's strict – that you don't meet the customers.'

'We don't,' said Julia, firmly. 'I've never met Captain Franks. But he sends me a few flowers, or a note when he's enjoyed the show.'

'Just old-world courtesy, I suppose.'

'He *has* asked me out to lunch but I haven't accepted – yet.'

38

'If he sends you notes often enough you will, no doubt.'

'Oh, Michael, don't. This is just silly.'

'God! I hope it is.' I pulled Julia into the brightly illuminated doorway of C. & A. and kissed her. I kissed her, screened from the street only by a lit shop-window full of skinny plastic models wearing busbies and showing their knees.

I kept kissing Julia, feeling her warm little body respond to mine, and I thought it was hell. It was hell because I hadn't been with a girl for almost a year.

'Michael!'

'Yes, love?'

'Michael, we're in *Oxford Street*.'

'Yes, I know.'

She pushed me away, gently. 'Michael, we *can't*!'

'It's quite respectable – in this blazing light.'

'Brrrow – brrrow –' *That* didn't sound like Julia.

'Oh, look!' She bent down and picked up the grey kitten that had been rubbing against our legs. 'It's a pet.'

'Brrrow.' The kitten hooked its claws into Julia's tweedcoat.

'This cat's a foreigner,' I told Julia.

'What do you mean?'

'It speaks English with an accent. It belongs to someone French or Italian.' At that moment a door across the street opened and a woman came out. '*Gatto-gatto-gatto!*' she called. '*Gatto-gatto! Vieni qui!*'

'Michael, how did you know?' Julia set down the kitten. It went shooting off towards the Italian voice.

'If animals are brought up with a foreign language or in a foreign country they learn different sounds.'

'Funny – I never thought of it. The dogs in India didn't sound like English dogs either. Let's go, Michael.'

The kitten had helped me; yet when we arrived at Julia's house in Baker Street I wanted her as much as ever. 'Darling, let me come in with you – I could do with a sandwich.'

'It's no good, Michael. My landlady would give me notice. She's –'

'I know – very strict; like Mr Malloy.'

'Worse; genteelly strict.' Julia stood on tiptoe and put her arms round my neck. Her body, at any rate, was against parting from mine. 'I'm allowed visitors up to five in the afternoon. My landlady believes there's a time and place for *everything*. Michael, will you come for lunch?'

'I'll try, but I have a surgery. And I don't believe in this thing about a time and place for everything, do you?'

Those odd midday hours with Julia were almost as chaste and tantalising as the brief interlude in Oxford Street; rather less magical in the dreary winter-light that filtered in between the drab rust-coloured chenille curtains.

Mrs Buller, the landlady, had an exasperating habit of getting flushed and girlish at the thought of 'young love'. She kept dropping in, offering Julia 'nice' things for our lunch, anything from her 'good' wine-glasses to remnants of her shepherd's pie.

How I should have liked to end the agony! But with my miserable salary, most of it about to be swallowed up by Uncle Simon's Silver Ghost, I did not want even to mention marriage. The time to think of that was at the end of my probation, with my partnership safe, and Julia – I hoped – as tired as I of working when we should have been together.

There was Winky's party. I especially wanted her to meet Claire and John, Winky and Tiger.

'Michael, I can't take a Saturday off,' she insisted. 'It's our busiest night at the *Purple Pigeon*.'

'Damn the *Purple Pigeon*.'

'It pays me fifty pounds a week.'

It was more than twice as much as I was earning. 'But surely the *Purple Pigeon* can do without you just for once.'

40

'No, I can't let Mr Malloy down,' said Julia. 'Many of our patrons come every Saturday night. They'd be disappointed if they didn't see Cobby.'

'Julia, you don't seriously believe they turn up regularly to see a *snake*?'

'Of course they do. Cobby's so clever – she always manages to look dangerous. They love that. Tell me about the party afterwards and I'll *imagine* what it was like. Anyway, who are these people?'

'Winky, Vincent Trail, is a cousin of Claire's.'

'Claire?'

'Claire Brown-Claremont.'

Julia stiffened, almost perceptibly. 'Wasn't she a debutante? The banker's daughter?'

'Yes. I'm looking after her siamese cats.'

'Oh, yes, I've read about them; purple, aren't they?'

'Lilac-pointed. Then there's Tiger; he has an antique shop in Chelsea. Claire works for him. And John Hooper; he's another friend of Claire's. I think they're neighbours in the country.'

'You've made some important friends. Useful to you.'

'That's what I think,' I told Julia. 'But I also happen to like them.'

'I'm sorry. I didn't mean to be bitchy.'

'I've *asked* you to come with me. Winky and Claire said they'd be delighted to have you.'

'Pity, I'm sure Cobby would be marvellous at a Chinese party.'

CHAPTER THREE

We were sitting on cushions on the floor of Winky's great entrance hall. In the centre stood a table of hot-plates keeping warm dishes of rice, chicken, lobster and curry. The guests helped themselves when they felt like eating.

'Of course, Winky's people have a lot of money,' said Molly, stretching her plump schoolgirl arms. 'This is luxury! Do you know they have three different kinds of toilet-paper in their penny-house – of course, I don't think the food tonight's much good.'

'Why not?'

'Well! Champagne and curry! *Aphrodisiacs!*'

If there were aphrodisiacs about the effect seemed mild enough. In the hall solemn groups of girls and young men, looking inevitably English in mandarin coats and Chinese tunics, were eating and talking; in the adjoining room someone had put on a record and a few couples were gyrating with earnest ferocity.

Molly looked at her watch. 'In ten minutes Tiger's going to read the first act of his play. It'll become a classic, you know. I am going to study English Literature.'

'Are you? Where?'

'Not at university, worse luck. By myself. I'd like to go to university but my parents can't afford it.'

'Haven't you got a place in the country?' I distinctly remembered John Hooper talking of Hazelbridge House and saying it had belonged to his family since the fifteenth century. And there was Uncle Dick, a member of the Royal Ouse Yacht Club.

'Oh, we've got Hazelbridge,' said Molly, indifferently.

'Well, then, surely you could go to university.'

'Can't afford it. It costs a fortune to keep a horse. We've got six.'

The music had stopped and the rest of the party came crowding into the hall. John and Winky went round distributing bottles of Coca-Cola.

Claire, in tight velvet trousers and a Chinese tunic, stood up and clapped her hands. 'Listen, everyone! In February Tiger's play will be put on at the Wellington Theatre. As a birthday present to Winky, Tiger's now going to read you the first act.' Tiger began:

'The scene is a cupboard under the stairs of the Millers' council house,' explained Claire in an off-stage murmur. 'Bob Miller has just come home from work. His wife is dusting jam jars . . .'

After five minutes or so listening to Tiger I began to wonder whether there was something wrong with me. Perhaps curry *was* an aphrodisiac, something that stimulated everything except my brain. London's richest and most famous impresario had described the play as the most profound to reach the West End in years but none of it meant a thing to me. The rest of the party was sitting there silent and spellbound, listening to Tiger with wide-awake eyes.

The act lasted three-quarters of an hour.

'Isn't it absolutely amazing!' exclaimed Molly, when the applause had subsided. 'The way Tiger shows how meaningless it all is!'

'Quite meaningless,' I said.

'Marvellous! It'll go like a bomb on Broadway.'

'You mean the Americans have bought this play?' I could scarcely conceal my incredulity.

'Yes, naturally.'

'Michael,' Claire squatted down beside me. 'Look, I don't want to break up the party, but I think I should go and see Chou-en-Lai.'

Pregnant pussies, I thought thankfully, that *was* something I understood. 'Want me to come?'

'Would you!'

'Didn't you manage to find a baby-sitter?'

'Oh, yes, Tiger's second-in-command's at the flat. But Bernard's a *man*. If Chou-en-Lai did start having her kittens he wouldn't know what to do. He might even forget to phone.'

I rang Claire on the following day.

'No change,' she said. 'But things are moving in her tummy, Michael. When will you come?'

'About eight?'

'All right. Have some dinner with us. John and Tiger will be here – wasn't it a marvellous party?'

'Marvellous – see you later, Claire.'

At half past eight Chou-en-Lai, watched by Mao-tse-Tung, was still dozing in front of the fire, placidly pregnant. At nine o'clock Tiger served us deep-frozen chips, sprouts and chops. Chops clearly haunted him both artistically and gastronomically; but neither Claire nor John seemed to have noticed that.

Over coffee in the lilac lounge Claire talked of Tiger's play; it distilled the very essence of life in the sixties – the aimlessness, the loneliness, the fatuity. The chop – all bone and no meat – was the very symbol of – 'Where's Chou?' she suddenly interrupted herself.

'She was here a moment ago,' said John.

'No,' said Tiger, 'I haven't seen her since we started dinner.'

It was time I went to meet Julia. 'Look inside the easter-egg,' I suggested.

Everyone looked everywhere.

'Oh, my God!' John's voice came from beyond the bathroom. 'No!'

We all rushed through into Claire's bedroom.

'Look!'

Chou-en-Lai lay embedded on a pile of magnificent silk mandarin coats. She had left the sticky ravages of birth for a cleaner section of the embroidery, and was licking four pink, naked kittens.

'Uncle Dick's coats!' groaned John. 'They're five hundred years old! How are we going to get the stains out?'

'Clever one!' Claire gently picked up Chou and carried her to a satin-quilted basket. 'There; isn't that better? Michael, *you'd* better lift the kittens. I don't want to hurt them – they're such tiny things.'

'Claire, the stains,' pleaded John.

'We'll get them out,' said Claire, absent-mindedly.

'How?'

'Cold water,' I suggested.

'Probably spoil the embroidery,' said Tiger. 'Claire, how about that little man we sometimes meet at the Crown – the manufacturer of society gloves.'

'Oh, Alfred Donizetti.'

'Didn't he say something about a reconditioning department, for taking stains out of gloves?'

'I think he did.'

'Ring him up,' begged John.

'He'll be in bed,' said Claire. 'It's after ten.'

It was, and I should have been at the coffee-bar meeting Julia.

'We can't wait until morning,' objected John. 'If we don't do something right away we'll never get those stains out. Claire, *please*.'

'Very well.' Claire reluctantly left Chou in my charge, and went to look up Donizetti's number. She dialled it on the phone beside her bed.

'*Pronto! Pronto!*' a man's voice came shouting through.

'Mr Donizetti?'

'*Si*, yes. Who is it?'

Claire explained, interrupted by a harsh voice at the other end complaining about women ringing up 'Alfredo' even at night, even with his wife beside him.

'He's coming,' said Claire, putting down the receiver.

'His wife didn't sound too pleased,' I said, thinking of the repercussions on Joanna.

'No.' Claire knelt down beside Chou-en-Lai's basket. 'Shall I send her one of the kittens, perhaps?'

'I don't think she'd appreciate it.'

'Oh, Michael! Weren't you going to meet Julia?'

'It's too late now.'

'You've been absolutely wonderful – and we almost forgot! John's Uncle Dick wants you to go and see his dog. John, write down his address for Michael. That'll be a new patient for your list, won't it?'

Julia was quite prepared to forgive me for not meeting her after the show. She sounded sweetly reasonable on the phone; *of course* I had to stay if it meant an introduction to a new patient; since my future depended on the number of new patients I could collect I'd been right not to neglect last night's opportunity. Who was the new patient? Anyone exciting?

I should have known better than to tell her it was John Hooper's uncle. She did not exactly accuse me of having spent a wild evening with Claire, but her voice became cool. She said she wouldn't wait for me that evening; she'd go home in Mr Malloy's van.

'But, darling, I know I can make it tonight,' I argued.

'No, I think I'll take the van, Michael. I don't like being on my own after the show; it isn't safe in Soho.'

'Did anything happen to you last night?'

'Not much.'

'Julia, what happened?'

'Oh, nothing.'

'Listen, I'll be meeting you. That's definite.'

'If one of Claire's cats isn't sick.'

'Don't be foolish, darling. You don't believe I *liked* letting you down!'

'No.' Julia sounded almost contrite.

'Well, what happened to you last night.'

'It really wasn't anything much. Don't worry.'

'I shall worry if you don't tell me.'

'Oh, some man tacked on to me when I left our coffee bar. So I took a taxi home.'

'He didn't –'

'Don't be silly. Do you know what he wanted?' Julia giggled.

'I can imagine.'

'Oh, no, you can't. He asked whether he could look at my *Evening Standard* – at the football results. It was all he did want.'

'You're unscrupulous, Julia.'

'Yes, darling – where you are concerned, Michael, but I *am* glad about your new patient.'

'His Grace will join you in a moment,' said the white-haired gentleman who had opened the door. 'His Grace' sounded distinctly peculiar in Queen's Gate, in a crammed flat on top of the house. John had given me the address but no name; I hadn't even noticed, thinking of my new animal-owner as John's Uncle Dick. 'In here if you please.' The gentleman led me into a bedroom and disappeared.

The room contained a Victorian hat-stand hung like a Christmas tree with dog-collars and leads, a couple of china bowls on the floor, and a single bed with a comfortably curled-up greyhound. I went to look at the labels on the dog-collars. The greyhound was Grey Rainbow, its owner – most oddly – a duke, the Duke of Alanspring.

47

I sat on the bed, and stroked the dog. It raised its head, sniffed, and subsided again. 'Up, Rainbow,' I encouraged him. 'Up, boy!' No reaction. 'You're too fat my lad.'

'Just what I say.' Another white-haired gentleman had come in, taller than the first and more rugged. The bony ledge of his forehead overhung a pair of bright blue eyes which surveyed the greyhound with a mixture of love and exasperation. 'My man Masters overfeeds the dog – told him he did.'

'How much exercise does Rainbow get?'

'Two hours a day. I take him out in the morning, Masters in the evening. He's a beautiful runner.' The Duke glared at me as if he expected contradictions.

'So he should be; he has the build.'

'That's what *I* say. You an expert on dog-racing?'

'No, not on racing.'

'Neither am I.' The Duke sounded wistful. 'That's our trouble. Too many crooks in the business.'

'Has Rainbow done much racing?'

'None, so far. I took him away from one track; didn't like the way they treated the dogs there. Didn't like the manager either. Last year we had him up at Woolchester, but they didn't let him run. If you ask me there was some funny business going on; the manager said his advice was not to enter Rainbow for racing at all. Wouldn't say more than that. Absolute rot! The dog's a beautiful runner. One only needs to look at him.'

'Well, I'll examine him.'

'You won't find anything wrong.'

I didn't. Rainbow's feet were perfect, no knock-up toes, the pelvis was normal, the muscle-tone was good. Apart from being too fat the dog was entirely sound.

'It's what I expected,' said the Duke. 'Want you to tell my sister. Come along, Lady Jane is next door.'

Lady Jane, a more elongated, more dry-skinned edition

of John and Molly, listened politely. Her thin, handsome face concealed the boredom she felt; her fingers twisting the wedding-ring plainly revealed her indifference to creatures such as Grey Rainbow.

'There, you see, Jane,' the Duke wound up, 'no reason why he shouldn't turn out a winner.'

'If you can get him on a race-track,' said Lady Jane, under her breath.

'What?'

'Well, Dick, you get his weight down,' said Lady Jane, 'as Mr Morton suggests – do you look after horses too, Mr Morton?'

'Certainly. I've spent the past four years in the country, looking after horses.' There seemed no point in mentioning the cattle, the sheep, and the small fry.

'Horses!' snorted the Duke.

'We recently lost our vet,' said Lady Jane.

'Fellow drank creme de menthe,' muttered his Grace. 'Grey Rainbow didn't like him.'

'A tragedy,' said Lady Jane. 'Now we haven't got a vet for our horses. Mr McGuire, the local man, can't look after them – except perhaps in an emergency; he's too busy with the Alderton Stables and the cattle. Would *you* be available at week-ends?'

'Yes, I think I could manage.'

'Splendid. We have two hunters and four ponies; Rustler's by Rust Arab out of Tudor Rose. The mare . . .' Lady Jane launched into the history of horses and ponies with an eloquence that sent the Duke to sleep.

An hour later, the moment her voice ceased, he jumped out of his chair as if he had been fully alert all the time. 'Must you really go, Morton? I'm sorry we kept you. I was hoping we'd discuss the future of Grey Rainbow. What we need is a *plan* – a *regimen* designed to get that dog on the race-track; in front of the other dogs, where he should be.

49

Don't you agree?'

'Of course.'

'Good man.' The Duke patted my shoulder. 'Tell you what; come and have lunch at my club. No distractions there.'

The Royal Ouse Yacht Club was empty, except for the two marble unicorns which guarded the famous stairway, the Duke, and an army of waiters. The waiters moved about the vast high-ceilinged rooms at just the right speed, with just the right air of formality-cum-familiarity; they were almost certainly ex-petty officers.

The Duke discussed Grey Rainbow's *regimen* over a glass of sherry, a plate of lukewarm oxo called consommé, over a dish of tired lamb stifled in disintegrated potatoes and sprouts. He explained to me what a dog like Grey Rainbow *should* be able to achieve while I chewed an immature suet-pudding and finally a piece of hardened mousetrap cheese. The coffee, pallid and lukewarm, was served to us in the green leather smoke-room to the sounds of a ship's clock with recurrent attacks of bronchial asthma. It was very peaceful.

'In two year's time,' said the Duke, 'all this will be gone.'

'The Club, sir?'

'We'll still have a club, probably on the top floor. But first they're going to pull the whole place down – even the stairway. They say the rooms are uneconomical.'

'I suppose there could be more than two floors.'

'There'll be six – mainly flats. Pity – too many speculators in the business. It's as bad as dog-racing. Still – you've got the right ideas for Rainbow. You can be sure I'll see to it that Masters doesn't overfeed him. And he'll get his four hours out if I have to walk him myself. When do you think we can try him out in the country?'

'As soon as his weight's down to what it should be.'

'We'll take him down to Hazelbridge.' The Duke's eyes closed, almost disappearing in the shadows of the over-hanging forehead. The clock had another heart-attack. The waiter, smiling at the dozing Duke, silently removed the coffee-tray. I thought we were sufficiently alone for me to waken my host without alarming the petty officers in the adjoining bar. I gave a low growl which sounded to me exactly like a greyhound's. No reaction. What kind of noise did a greyhound make on smelling a hare? A high-pitched yelp, as far as I could remember.

My second yelp succeeded. His Grace shot upright in his chair. 'Know anything about sailing?' he asked briskly.

'Not a great deal,' I admitted, conscious of the oil-paint-ings of yachts round the walls. 'But I like boats.'

'I don't,' said the Duke. 'What *I* was interested in was lawn-mowers – wind-driven, you understand. We don't use air currents nearly as much as we should. It's a shocking waste – yes, I used to think a lot could be done with wind-driven lawn-mowers.'

'It's ingenious.'

'A dead loss,' the Duke shook his head, 'commercially.'

The subject appeared to be dismissed. I asked, 'What are the conditions for joining the Royal Ouse Yacht Club, sir?'

'Conditions? Oh, you must be able to pay the subscrip-tion. Fifty pounds. Or you can become an associate member for twenty-five. Want to join?'

'Not just yet, sir.'

'It's too dear, I agree. They put up the subscription twice in the past five years. Of course I'm only an associate. Not much good, you know, if you can't afford to be a full member – can't use the residential wing; best part of the Club.'

'If one doesn't live in London.'

'I want to give up my flat,' said the Duke, 'take a room at the Club for Rainbow, a room for myself – send Masters

51

down to the cottage in Hazelbridge; fellow doesn't like the city. Time he retired.' The Duke leaned forward. 'There's only one fly in the ointment, Morton. I can't afford it. Been living on capital for years. Only *one* solid asset left – Grey Rainbow.'

'I wouldn't say *any* greyhound's a *solid* asset.'

'Rainbow is, Morton. Wait till you see him in the country. Incidentally, what are you going to charge me?'

'The usual fees,' I said, cautiously.

'Well – Rainbow's worth it. It'll be different in the country, won't it? You'll be looking after my sister's horses in any case.'

I was beginning to wonder whether Lady Jane and the Duke *would* qualify as 'new regularly attended animal-owners' according to the agreement between myself and Uncle Simon. My uncle would not accept an expansion of the practice without an expansion of income. How much would the income of the practice increase with a Duke whose only 'solid' asset was a greyhound and a horse-owner too broke to send her daughter to university?

'You'll have no expenses in Hazelbridge,' the Duke assured me. 'You'll be staying at my sister's. Think she'll invite you for Christmas.'

CHAPTER FOUR

'Christmas with the Hoopers might be a mistake,' Muriel agreed with me, somewhat reluctantly. 'Though it's a time when it's fun to be with a family.'

'Christmas with the Hoopers *would* be a mistake,' I told her. I helped her collect the instruments which were scattered about the surgery, and switched on the steriliser. 'They'd regard me as a friend of the family ever after. And friends don't send bills – if they do it's considered bad taste. I'm staying in London.'

'Well, we'll have the Donizettis on Christmas Day, as usual.' Muriel stripped the operating table and covered it with a clean sheet. 'I must get candles for Joanna's tree, and –'

'On Boxing Day I'm taking you out for dinner – launch your new hairstyle.'

'Nonsense!' Muriel touched her hair, now soft, smooth and silver blue. 'You should be asking Julia.'

'Julia will be snake-dancing. If she weren't I'd take both of you out.'

'There's no need, Michael.'

'None at all; that's why we'll enjoy ourselves.'

Muriel ran the water in the wash-basin and began to clean it. 'I went mad, Michael,' she said, keeping her back to me. 'After the hairdressers yesterday I . . . I bought shoes . . . with rather high heels.'

'Let me see them.'

'Oh, not now.'

'Come on, Muriel, where are they?'

'I'll wear them at Christmas – on Boxing Day, perhaps.'

'We're going out whatever happens, Muriel.'

She turned sharply. 'Then you *are* worried about Andy!'

'Yes. The leg's mended surprisingly well for such an old dog. But I didn't like his smell. I bet he's incontinent.'

'Miss Shaw didn't say so.'

'Miss Shaw would ascribe it to old age.'

'The dog's been smelly for years,' said Muriel, hopefully.

'Yes, but the smell has changed since *I* have been treating Andy. I think one of his kidneys is damaged; it might even be both.'

'So he's dying?'

'I don't know yet. Andy's a strange little creature; he doesn't tell you when he's in pain. If he were younger – if he had a better heart I'd operate. I'd remove a kidney if the other were sound.'

'Wouldn't it be worth trying – even if he only lived a few months afterwards?'

'Even if Andy survived the operation – I don't think he would – he'd suffer. The pain would be worse than it is at the moment. I wish I had the guts to tell Miss Shaw that Andy should be put to sleep.'

'I know,' said Muriel. 'Your uncle used to put it off until the last moment.'

I could not face that last moment alone. The morning before Christmas I went along to Tiger's shop and begged one of Claire's kittens. Young as it was its parentage was already recognisable in the tabby markings of the body, the siamese features of the head and the distinctive blue of its half-open eyes.

The Archway Road was full of people carrying heavy baskets and Christmas trees; the shop-windoes were gaudy with gifts, all except the health-food shop which still displayed the same anaemic nuts in splitting packets and the same variety of dusty vinegar bottles.

As I opened the door beside the shop Miss Shaw came down the stairs. She was coming down much too quickly for her age.

'Oh, Doctor!' she said, breathlessly. 'I was just going to telephone you – I didn't want to trouble you but Andy is – there seems something wrong with him.'

'He wasn't well yesterday,' I told her, hating the unavoidable brutality. 'Let's take a look at him.'

Andy was lying in the smelly little room on Miss Shaw's bed. Water dribbling out of his blind eyes was staining the eiderdown, and his breath was coming in short, laboured gasps.

'It's his heart playing him up, Doctor, isn't it? Perhaps if you gave him something to quieten him down –'

I put the box with the kitten on her table. 'I brought you a Christmas present, Miss Shaw.' As I unfolded the piece of blanket inside the kitten stretched and yawned. It looked as charming as any mongrel kitten I'd ever seen.

Miss Shaw did not seem to notice it. 'Then Andy's dying,' she said, quietly. 'Doctor – is he dying?'

'I'm afraid so. I want you to let me take him away. You know, he's been in pain the past few days; not *bad* pain, but now it would get worse. I think we should make the end easy for him.'

Miss Shaw sat down beside the dog and stroked his head. She softly ran her hand over his trembling flanks. 'We've been together since my sister died – it'll be fifteen years next week – I'm being selfish Andy, aren't I. Doctor, I'm sure you know what's best for him. I don't want Andy to have a bad time. If you say he should be put to sleep –'

'Not here. I'll take him away with me.'

'Yes, Doctor,' she said, in a flat voice. 'Thank you. You've been very good to Andy. He won't be frightened, will he?'

'I promise you he won't. Miss Shaw, there's some food for the kitten in the box; minced meat and gravy.'

'The kitten?' Miss Shaw was still stroking Andy. 'Don't think I'm not grateful, Doctor, but I – I don't think I want another animal.'

'Nobody wants this little cat.' I held it up in one hand so that its forepaws groped in the air. 'It hasn't got a home. There are so many cats that don't get a chance of growing up; I thought it would be a pity to get rid of this one. It's rather special – half tabby, half siamese. Someone who's good with animals could make something of it – train it to walk on a lead.'

'Like a dog?' The helpless paws of the kitten were beginning to assert an effect.

'Certain breeds like walking on a lead.' I took the kitten back to the box. 'But I don't want to impose on your kindness, Miss Shaw – you don't want this little fellow; I understand.' I tightened my hold on the kitten and it gave, as I had hoped, a plaintive mew.

'Oh! poor pussy!' exclaimed Miss Shaw. 'I *will* keep him, Doctor. It would be a shame to put him to sleep, a pretty little thing like that.'

Having persuaded Miss Shaw not to see Andy off, I was making him comfortable in the car when she came rushing down to the street, the kitten tucked inside her coat.

'Doctor, I quite forgot.' She gave me a parcel wrapped in holly-sprigged paper. 'I made this for you, for Christmas.' Before I could thank her she was darting back into the house. '– nothing much, Doctor.'

It was a knitted muffler, at least six feet long, in several shades of lilac and mauve.

Julia's serpent abandoned the clockwork rabbit and concentrated on my muffler. Every time Cobby frisked at the muffler the muffler shifted. Cobby was intrigued; she was certain the long lilac thing was a snake, though somewhat different from herself; not as friendly. The clockwork rabbit wasn't half as much fun. I was pleased because the rabbit, together with six half-bottles of champagne for Julia, had been a Christmas present from the ubiquitous Captain Franks.

'I *haven't* met him,' said Julia, pouring me another glass of champagne. 'And I'm sure he doesn't really expect to meet me. Captain Franks regards the *Purple Pigeon* as a sort of club. Bill says he meets his friends in the bar – now stop talking about him, darling. Don't spoil things.'

'Things' were delightful with Mrs Buller away on holiday; we had the flat to ourselves and there was no danger of anyone 'dropping in'.

Julia stretched out on the couch beside me, her bare brown legs intertwining with mine. She'd once told me that she hated having her legs covered; I hoped she'd go on hating it. I liked her best in shorts or in her velvet vine-leaves with one of her respectable cardigans on top and a pair of fur-slippers on her feet. And when her long black hair was loose, spilled out over her face and shoulders, she looked like a miniature of Tarzan's wife. I'd once been in love with Tarzan's wife almost as much as I was now in love with Julia.

'Michael, I won't be able to go to the Armstrongs' party with you,' she said, 'but we can meet afterwards.'

'The party's at six – you could manage that, surely.'

'Well, I *thought* I could, but we're doing an early show this evening – you know, a Christmas show.'

'What, nudes with angels' wings!'

'Don't be absurd, Michael. The girls are going to wear gowns – long, transparent ones. There's going to be a manger, the three kings, animals –'

'You and Cobby?'

'Do be serious! It's going to be a religious show – a kind of nativity mime.'

'For the elders of Mr Malloy's kirk?'

'I don't know why you're so unkind about him. He takes

57

the *Purple Pigeon* very seriously.'

'And the money it makes.'

'The money from the nativity show is going to the Presbyterian Church. No, it's useless arguing with you about Mr Malloy; you just haven't anything in common.'

'Luckily for *me*.' I brushed away the heavy curtain of hair and kissed her. Cobby darted forward and reared her head. Though she came to me amicably enough when I whistled her favourite tune, 'On Ilkley Moor baht 'at,' that snake was jealous.

'I'll be free about eight,' said Julia, fondling the snake's back.

'I'll be free all evening if there's no emergency. Shall I ring you?'

'No, I tell you what – I'll take a taxi to Knightsbridge; I'd like to see your local.'

'All right, the Crown, then. Muriel will give us supper later.'

'You'd better eat something before you go out; by way of blotting paper.'

'Have a *benedictine* – have a *strega* – have a *millefiore*.' Alfred Donizetti dumped a whole collection of exotic bottles on the marble-mosaic table in front of the semi-circular couch. 'Or a *chanchullo* . . .'

'Alfredo, really!' Mrs Donizetti got up, and began returning the bottles to the cocktail cabinet. 'You *can't* offer your guests liqueurs at five in the afternoon. I'm going to serve hot *pizza* – open a bottle of wine.' She swept out, dark and majestic, leaving her husband utterly deflated.

Muriel smiled. 'Your new furniture's quite perfect in this room, Mr Donizetti. Joanna said you chose it yourself.'

Joanna, with the absorbed, withdrawn look of a lonely child, was kneeling on a chair by the window whispering to her thrush. The bird was talking back, twittering softly as if

58

sitting on a tree in the country on a summer evening.

'You like Italian table?' Alfred's dark eyes had become animated. 'Is made by good artist in Firenze.'

'Yes, it's lovely – so is this couch. I think you're very clever.'

He shrugged his shoulders. 'I know about fashion-things, Mrs Whiting – is my business. But the clever one is my wife – she is not like me – just foreigner. Carlotta had Italian parents too, but she is born in England. She attend good school – learned the English life –'   ..

'You didn't have to learn,' said Muriel. 'You know a beautiful thing when you see it. Your house proves that.'

'Thank you, thank you.' Donizetti beamed at us. 'Ah, but the house is cold, no? It is the Number Seven beside us, empty all the time. Carlotta says we pay for the heating of the Number Seven. Why you not buy, Mr Michael?'

'I can't afford it.'

'Is great pity. Joanna would like – eh, *piccola?* Oh, is terrible my English! Beg your pardon. You know what happened? President of glove-maker society ask me to speak after the dinner. I am very frightened; my knees go funny. So I say, "Ladies and gentlemen. Tonight we've ate good English dinner. I like what is English and I love the English language, and now I will speak to you in Italian." '

Even Joanna was laughing when Mrs Donizetti returned, carrying a platter of hot *pizza*.

'Is good cook, my wife,' said Alfred, 'you eat plenty, Mr Michael. Is always the gin at English parties; you eat plenty *pizza* before you go to the cocktails.'

'The cocktails' in London were as hazardous as the cock-tails of a country practice. As usual trades and press, churches, clubs and societies had whipped up millions of pounds' worth of goodwill so that even my teetotal animal-lovers had felt they should buy 'something to drink at

Christmas.'

Muriel and I had received dozens of 'At Home' cards and as many telephone invitations asking us to 'drop in for a drink.' Muriel had charted the houses she would visit on behalf of Uncle Simon, the invitations I would have to accept, and the houses where a visitor was something of a special event.

After wine and *pizza* with the Donizettis I went back to the Archway Road to tell Miss Shaw of Andy's untroubled end, and to make sure the kitten was taking over. It was; sufficiently well to keep Miss Shaw from sitting still and noticing Andy's absence *all* the time. Miss Shaw gave me a glass of some powerful dandelion wine.

I had to have sherry with another old lady who owned a pekinese, a gin and tonic with a couple of cat-addicts, a pink gin with a man who kept tropical fish, and whisky with a television naturalist who kept tortoises under his bed and terrapins in his bath.

By the time I got to Harley Street my tongue was hanging out for a quenching pint of beer. It was the one thing Dr Armstrong was not offering me. His guests were on champagne or martini. To do the Armstrongs justice beer would have been out of place in their pale blue and white drawing-room, in the hands of guests who wore their best drinking-suits or shimmering dresses with fragile shoes.

I took special note of the women's shoes; I thought Muriel would be pleased to hear that the guests at the most luxurious house on our list had been wearing the kind of shoes she herself had bought, shoes with very high heels made, as far as I could see, of dozens of thin layers of wood or leather.

'A word with you, Michael,' said Dr Armstrong, 'Before you get caught up in this scrum.' He zestfully took my arm. 'Come down to the consulting room. I want your advice – you don't mind, do you?'

Perhaps it was part of Peter Armstrong's psychiatric

technique that one didn't mind giving him free advice at unlikely hours. His thin little figure was constantly on the move, the short-sighted boyish face always animated; and he rarely stopped talking.

'Elizabeth's Christmas present may be a bit of a headache,' he said, hustling me down the stairs to his ground-floor consulting room. 'I've been watching her lately; I think she's developing a complex. As you know she's awfully good with our fox . . . she really has an understanding of wild creatures – but I've come to the conclusion that she wants something more docile – a cat, I'd say. The other night I actually heard her say something about a *pussy* in her sleep. Naturally I don't want her to develop a traumatic condition – so' – he flung open the door of his room – 'here it is!'

It was an attractive white long-hair cat with a round head, a silky frill round the neck and a bushy tail.

'Nicky,' said Peter Armstrong. 'I don't care for cats, but this one's quite engaging; pedigree animal, registered with the Governing Council of the Cat Fancy. Think my wife will like it?'

'I'm sure Elizabeth will be delighted.'

'Well, now, the problem's *Renard*. He hasn't seen this creature yet. I wanted you to be present when they meet – we can only have the cat if Renard will put up with it. Elizabeth would be shattered if he ate the puss.' Peter walked over to the far side of the room and opened a door. 'Come on, Renn – come on, old chap!'

The fox put his head round the corner, his body low to the ground. I noticed he'd been biting his tail again. Presumably Elizabeth had been too busy with preparations for her party to bathe Renard's tail in tonic-eater.

'Careful!' called Peter. 'Watch he doesn't make a dive for the cat.' The fox slunk round the walls, sniffing. 'You can never tell with a wild beast like this. He regards this as *his* house – he may try to kill the cat or he mightn't even notice her, out of pride.'

Renard did notice the white cat. He stalked round her, sniffed, and finally lowered himself on his belly, creeping nearer inch by inch. The cat, its amber eyes round and guileless, sat still and watched. Peter stood poised, ready to save the cat's life. When the fox was within a foot of the cat his breathing became agitated, he hesitated a moment, then suddenly made a leap forward which brought him face to face with the cat. Before either of us could grab Renard the cat had risen on its hindlegs, its front paws belabouring Renard's head.

The fox gave a pitiful yelp and took refuge under the desk.

'Extraordinary!' Peter went down on his knees. 'She didn't scratch Renard – no damage at all. Renard, I'm ashamed of you! Running away from a puss that can't even be bothered to show its claws. You see, Michael, that's what city life does – even to wild beasts.'

'Yes, isn't it lucky there are psychiatrists in London!'

Peter laughed. 'Well, isn't it? Anyway – now we know; the puss can look after itself. It should be all right to keep Nicky, don't you think?'

'*This* fox won't eat her.'

'It's a relief; I think Elizabeth really does need the cat – come along, Michael, we're wasting valuable drinking-time.'

The party had got under way judging by the voices which had markedly risen during the past half hour. Peter handed me a glass of champagne, Elizabeth was flinging names at me; Lord Whenderson – Mr Caple, who recently won the by-election at – Amanda Almacides, the famous novelist – Lady Smythe, Chairman of the Royal Commission for – Dr Crosby –

'I dare say treating animals isn't very different from treating people,' said Dr Crosby. 'Do you use antibiotics?'

'Yes, a good deal,' I told him. 'Except that in veterinary

work one mostly gives injections.'

'How awful!' exclaimed Lady Smythe. 'Sticking needles in dumb animals. I'd hate it. Of course, I can't bear injections myself. They always give me a headache, though I do appreciate how wonderful these new drugs are. Come to think of it medicine has made enormous strides –' She rattled on, platitude upon earnest platitude; they came out with a conviction that made them sound almost original.

Amanda Almacides yawned. 'The Chairman of the Royal Commission,' she murmured in my ear. 'How loathsome these Royal Commissions are! The female members so often are – well, a species of superannuated girls – detained at Roedean longer than was good for them.'

Wherever the lady-novelist had been detained it was not Roedean. Her platinum hair was done in the latest 'young' style, her face made up in pale flattering colours, obviously with great skill and knowledge.

'Nancy was telling me you've almost completed the William Laud biography,' she said, bending so close that I could see the age and the sadness somewhere between her beautiful bones and her beautiful make-up. 'When will it be published?'

'I'm not an author,' I said, quite guiltily. There is something uncomfortably pathetic about women who are too vain to wear their spectacles.

Miss Almacides absentmindedly stared at Lady Smythe. 'I'm glad. It was time *someone* wrote the biography of William Laud. He was the only Archbishop of Canterbury impeached of high treason who was beheaded – at least, I don't think any of the others were.'

'. . . in that doping case,' Lady Smythe was saying. 'Mr Morton, do tell us, do you think the *jockey* had anything to do with doping those two horses? Mrs Leyland, who owns some of the best steeplechasers in Ireland told me –'

'. . . happened with one of my first patients,' Dr Crosby

was telling Lord Whenderson. 'House-physicians in those days were paid the princely sum of fifty pounds per annum. So I took a second job, part-time work with a family doctor. The woman came into the surgery; there was no doubt in my mind, it was a case of shingles. She was quite offended – didn't believe me. I suppose I did look young and green. So she went to a foreign doctor who *didn't* stick his neck out; he just gave her a note to take along to the hospital – told her she'd see a specialist. So, off she went to the hospital, waited her turn in the out-patients' department, walked into the consulting room and *there* was the specialist – it so happened that *I* was on duty that day.' Dr Crosby's laughter boomed out, its impetus collecting a half dozen chuckles and smiles.

'The *Leylands* should know,' argued Lady Smythe. 'I'm not suggesting they've ever doped *their* horses – Mr Morton, do tell us, what is the drug they use for doping, nowadays?'

'Probably Prednisolone,' I told her. 'It's a synthetic cortisone.'

'I can't understand why such a thing is produced.'

Miss Almacides managed to focus her eyes on Lady Smythe. 'It's obvious,' she said, coldly. 'No doubt Prednisolone is also used as a cure.'

I thought our hostess was looking anxious. Though detained by a voluble matriarch Elizabeth kept glancing across the crowded room at Miss Almacides and Lady Smythe. It was possible they'd hated one another for many years, or it could have been that Elizabeth knew by experience how unlikely it was that Miss Almacides and Lady Smythe would relish one another's company.

Elizabeth suddenly plunged into the crowd and disappeared among people's legs. Presently the fox came dodging out, with Elizabeth in pursuit. He evaded her clutching hands and disappeared under a chair.

Elizabeth, now looking flushed as well as anxious, joined our group. 'Michael,' she whispered. 'I'm afraid Renard's

64

been misbehaving. Do you think I should –'

I heard a gasp beside me followed by a terrified scream. There was a scuffle, a frantic whirl of limbs which suddenly resolved into an amazing spectacle; Miss Almacides in the arms of Lady Smythe, clinging on as if in desperate need of protection; Lady Smythe slowly tilting backwards into the arms of Dr Crosby, and Dr Crosby sinking against Lord Whenderson's ample chest. I followed Elizabeth's helpless gesture towards the floor; in a confusion of legs I saw a couple of stiletto-heels chewed off as if they had been attacked by an army of termites.

'Renard,' whispered Elizabeth, helping Lady Smythe to her feet. 'Peter,' she appealed to her husband, 'he's under that chair. Get him!'

'Don't worry, darling. If he's under a chair he won't do any more damage.' He watched their guests pick each other up. 'Michael, you're wanted on the phone.'

'Very pretty, these thin heels,' I heard Dr Crosby hold forth, as I was making my way out, 'but quite absurd. It's a wonder they don't cause more accidents –'

'But it's fantastic!' exclaimed Lady Smythe. 'My right heel *and* Miss Almacides' left snapping off –'

I saw a movement by the chair and grabbed. Renard's teeth just grazed my hand, but I managed to catch him by the scruff, bundling him out unobserved except by Elizabeth.

'Very strange,' Miss Almacides agreed, amiably. 'Breaking at precisely the same moment. Lady Smythe, where did you get *your* shoes? It would be interesting . . .'

'Oh, so you *are* around,' said the small, disagreeable voice on the phone.

'Yes, Mrs Topper?' This, I decided, was one animal-owner I'd sack the moment my partnership was in the bag.

'Your Mrs Whiting wasn't exactly forthcoming, I must say.'

'She gave you this number, didn't she?'

'Not willingly. It may be Christmas but that's no reason why my poor dog should die of neglect.'

'What's the trouble, Mrs Topper?'

'I want you to come at once. I'm very worried about Pooky.'

I'd seen the little poodle less than a week ago; he'd been perfectly fit except for mild symptoms of hysteria which, as usual I'd stopped with a smack on his bottom. 'What's Pooky up to now?'

'You don't sound over-concerned, do you?' Mrs Topper's voice diminished even more. It became as thin as the fluting of wind over ice. 'How soon will you be here?'

'Mrs Topper, what's happened to your dog?'

'I can't discuss it over the phone.'

'I'd like to have *some* idea.'

'I said, I can't discuss it on the telephone. The whole thing is too embarrassing. It's monstrous!'

'Very well. I'll be along in half an hour.'

Some of Peter Armstrong's guests were drifting into the hall, Lord Whenderson jovially supporting Lady Smythe with one arm, Miss Almacides with the other. Both were carrying the savaged remains of their heels.

'My dear Amanda,' Lady Smythe was saying. 'I insist – I absolutely insist. Geoffrey, do tell her she *must* have dinner with us; we're not going without her.'

'So sweet of you, Cynthia –'

'Peter,' Elizabeth caught her husband's sleeve. 'Is Renard locked up?'

'Yes, darling. Don't worry.'

'It's been a gorgeous party; Elizabeth, darling, we must meet –'

'Sorry you have to go, Michael,' said Peter. 'Elizabeth

ould like a post-mortem on the party – that's what she enjoys best. Sure you won't stay for another drink?'

'No, I said I'd be in Hampstead in half an hour.'

'Too bad. An emergency?'

'Maybe a case for a psychiatrist.'

'Now you'll believe me, perhaps.' Mrs Topper's voice rose to a nervous shout that made her husband jump out of his chair. 'It's not a predicament one can discuss over the phone, is it? Pooky darling, come to mummy!'

Pooky was feeling too miserable to come to anyone. He was sitting on the edge of the persian carpet, hiding behind a coffee-table, head down, ears drooping, crying to himself softly, from discomfort and not hysteria. His sexual organ and glands were protruding from their sheath, obviously unable to return.

'How long has he been like this?' I asked.

'Since the morning, poor darling.'

'What he needs,' said Mr Topper, 'is a *four-legged* bitch.'

'Archibald, Mr Morton hasn't asked you for advice.' Mrs Topper picked up her poodle, and he immediately tried to struggle free. 'Mr Morton, is it sometimes serious?'

'No, it's simply an erection.'

'I told you, Mary,' said Mr Topper. 'Males do have erections, though you seem to notice it in dogs only.'

'Archibald! Please!'

'Small dogs are particularly prone to such accidents,' I said, quickly. 'Pooky got over-excited –'

'Not surprisingly.' Mr Topper's aggressive mood was something new to me. It was as embarrassing as his wife's rudeness.

'Where can we immerse Pooky in water?' I asked.

'Water?' Mrs Topper let go the struggling poodle. 'Water seems to be the mainstay of your treatments – though I'll admit *I* sometimes go abroad for a water-cure.'

67

'Not for the same reason,' muttered Mr Topper.

'Shall we take Pooky to the kitchen?'

'Certainly not; he has his own bath – Archibald, go and fill it up with warm water.'

'Cold water,' I said.

'With cold water,' agreed Mr Topper, with alacrity.

'Poor darling – Archibald, bring the bath in here. The least we can do is to treat Pooky in front of the fire. And *please* take out your cat.'

Pooky yelped when I immersed his hindquarters in the cold bath, but his sex organs retracted almost at once, and when I stroked him his ears went up. I gave him five grains of the potassium bromide I'd picked up on my way to Hampstead, and he fell asleep almost at once.

'Well,' said Mrs Topper. 'How much are you going to charge me for that?'

'Ten pounds.'

'The treatment wasn't exactly complicated, was it? I could have done as much myself.'

'Yes,' I agreed. 'But you didn't wish to discuss Pooky's accident over the telephone.'

Mrs Topper didn't answer. Out came her large, grubby Woolworth bag with the crumpled pound notes.

'You've had a lesson in natural history, Mary,' said Mr Topper. 'In future you'll recognise an erection when you see one. Cheap at the price, eh?'

'Archibald, you revolt me.' Mrs Topper flung me the money, and fled from the room.

'Have a drink,' said Topper.

'No, thanks – I've had a social day of it.' I wound Miss Shaw's lilac muffler round my neck and picked up my gloves.

'Where are you going now?'

It was asked so wistfully that I couldn't refuse an answer. 'The Crown, in Knightsbridge.'

'Your local pub? Hang on, I'm coming with you.'

'But I'm meeting a girl.'

'Won't be long!' shouted Topper, striding into the hall. 'I'm just changing my shoes – help yourself to a drink.'

Topper tossed back a half dozen double whiskies to my two half pints of beer. From the moment he'd said 'there's money in it, but God how I hate Christmas' I knew I was in for a tale of all his Christmases. It was as Uncle Simon had said: beware of women who call their dogs darling and their husbands by the full Christian name. This husband was none of my business but as Simon had warned me, there was a danger he soon would be. I couldn't see him get home under his own steam if he kept knocking back doubles.

His was a sad and not exactly original story: boy meets poor little rich girl, girl exchanges her money for 'understanding,' husband uses wife's money for building up a business, wife reminds husband he'd have been in the gutter without *her* money, husband goes on a binge and meets wonderful girl, husband happy – wife suspicious, wife discovers all, wife threatens scandal involving wonderful girl, husband capitulates, wife becomes poodle-owner and top-dog.

The bar, all softly lit mahogany and polished brass, was quiet. Presumably the usual customers had hustled home their purchases from Harrods and Harvey Nichols, the Scotch House and Woollands, and were wrapping them in holly-sprigged paper.

Maybe Christmas was commercialised – that saying had become quite a chestnut – but the goodwill of my animal-owners had been genuine in most cases. I wasn't doing too badly. With three months of my probation-year completed I had not yet lost a single one of Simon's regular animal-owners, not even Mrs Topper, and I'd gained a promising nucleus of new ones: a Duke with white-hot hopes in his greyhound, Claire with her lilac-pointed cats and matching flat, the horse-owning Hoopers and, of course, Julia. The question was, would Julia and her serpent come within the terms of my agreement with Simon if I asked her to marry me? I decided it would be safer not to count her as a new regularly attended animal-owner, no matter how regularly I attended her.

'S'a mar-vellous creature,' said Topper, thickly. 'S'matter of fact s'a whole lot of marvellous creatures . . . look!' he extended a wavering index finger, 'there!'

Tiger had come in, ginger beard and freckles above ginger sheepskin coat, and Claire in her shaggy lilac pants and a purple anorak with Chou-en-Lai round her neck.

'Puss puss,' Topper called, 'nice pushy –'

'Hello, Michael!' Claire and Tiger came to our table and sank wearily into a couple of red leather chairs.

'What a day!' groaned Tiger. 'Turned over and trampled by the frenzied mob.'

'A mob with big wallets,' said Claire, contentedly. 'You should have seen Tiger's shop; it was a riot. Amazing what people will buy as Christmas gifts – Victorian hall-seats, French china wash-bowls, fans, jerries, whatnots –'

'Bob!' Tiger signalled the waiter, 'two Coca-Cola – what will you have, Michael? – half a pint of bitter; and for you, Mr –'

'Tooper.'

'Coca-Cola,' I ordered.

'S'right,' Topper nodded violently. 'My friend knows best – s'a great thing a friend who understands evvy-thing.'

'What a gorgeous thing!' exclaimed Claire, picking up Miss Shaw's muffler. 'Michael, is it yours?' She put Chou-en-Lai on her lap and the muffler round her neck. 'Do look, Tiger. Isn't it perfect? The same colours as my trousers and sweater.'

'It does go frightfully well,' agreed Tiger.

Claire was cuddling the muffler, making ecstatic little

70

noises, rather like Chou-en-Lai at her feeding-bowl. I had to admit that the thing looked better on Claire than on myself. 'Keep it,' I said, 'as a Christmas present.'

'Michael, you *are* a pet! Tiger, let's give him our present.' My present, which Tiger extracted from the depths of his sheepskin coat, was a folder of Chinese pictures of cats which looked much like Mao-tse-Tung and Chou-en-Lai. They were painted on silk, obviously old and valuable. I admired my present and thanked Tiger and Claire.

'Rather interesting, these things,' said Tiger. 'Painted – I'd say by Yuan Yu-Tai – during the early Ming Dynasty. I bought this lot from the Maharanee of Madurapore.'

Claire was gazing at Tiger with touching admiration, which he either took for granted or didn't notice. 'No one in London knows as much as Tiger about Chinese antiques,' she told Topper. 'You must come and see our shop in Chelsea.'

'Most certainly.' Topper sounded defiant. 'What I want is pictures of pussies – hundreds of pussies. I'm going to hang pussies all over my house. I love pussies. Now, my wife –'

Before he could launch into a repetition of the boy-meets-poor-little-rich-girl story Julia came flying into the bar and I went to meet her.

'Darling, I'm so sorry I'm late.' She had brought in a whiff of sweet, frosty air. 'I walked most of the way – couldn't get a taxi until I got to Green Park – oh, you're here with a party.'

As soon as I'd introduced her, Topper picked her for his soul-mate. She was, he declared, so like a girl he'd known – a most wonderful woman. If it hadn't been for his wife's habit of . . .

Topper's voice droned on. Tiger was telling me about a sale at Sotheby's where he'd picked up a Famille Noire vase. Claire, still excited about the flourishing Christmas-business, was talking about the customers who had all but wrecked

71

Tiger's tasteful displays.

At ten o'clock they suddenly made up their minds they wanted something more nourishing than the Crown's steak-pies, and got up. Instead of wearing Chou-en-Lai round her neck, as usual, Claire put the cat in the pocket of her anorak and draped the lilac muffler over her head and shoulders.

I saw Julia's neck arch, not unlike her snake's when it was about to spit. 'What a nice muffler, Claire.'

'Yes, isn't it beautiful,' said Claire, warmly. 'If Michael had ordered it specially for me it couldn't –'

'I'm sure Michael did order it specially.' Julia's grey eyes glittered with angry tears. 'Have a good time, everyone.' She took Topper by the arm and somehow managed to make him stand up. 'Come on, Archie; we're going to *celebrate*.'

I took Julia's fingers. 'Darling, don't be silly. You don't –'

'Oh, yes!' she snatched her hand away. 'I do understand – very well.' She tucked Topper's arm in hers, and marched him out.

I was not going to run after her; I hoped 'celebrating' with someone as canned as Topper was would teach her a lesson. But I don't suppose I looked happy.

'Oh, Michael,' said Claire, 'I've dropped a brick, haven't I?'

'Have you?' asked Tiger, gazing at the floor as if looking for it. 'Weren't they going to eat with us?'

Claire, for once, ignored him. 'Michael, I *am* sorry. Will you be able to explain to Julia? Or should I –'

'It's all right,' I told her. 'Julia will come round.'

Julia didn't come round. All through Christmas Day I phoned the flat in Baker Street. There was no reply. There was no reply from the flat on Boxing Day and the telephone of the *Purple Pigeon* was permanently engaged. When I went to the *Purple Pigeon* in the evening Number One pugilist told me Julia wasn't dancing; he thought she had 'flu. Bill told me, in confidence, that Julia had gone home to Leamington Spa; what worried Mr Malloy was that she'd taken her snake.

I telephoned half a dozen Hanleys in and around Leamington Spa until a Major Hanley confirmed that he had a daughter and a snake. Julia, he told me, had arrived home on Christmas Day but she'd left the following morning because she was starting a new job in Scotland. No, he didn't have her address. All he knew was that she would be a physical training instructress with a travelling National Dances and Cultures Society.

After an appalling night, when I dreamed of Julia dancing naked before a howling mob in Liverpool docks, of Julia being crushed in a writhing knot of serpents, of Julia in my arms turning into a hissing cobra, I telephoned Topper.

He sounded his usual grey self. Miss Julia Hanley? No, he couldn't remember anyone by that name. When I reminded him of the Crown and of Christmas Eve he became somewhat reserved. He hadn't felt too well, he told me; he believed some young lady had very kindly persuaded him to have something to eat. After that, he really couldn't say. He'd gone home in a taxi.

Muriel was sympathetic but not altogether on my side. She let me know I'd behaved foolishly, to say the least. Not only had I worn the purple muffler, telling Julia the story of Miss Shaw and Andy, not only had I given it away to another girl, but I had done so before giving Julia *her* Christmas present. I felt worse for not even having bought a present for Julia.

In a moment of madness I felt convinced my dream had been prophetic and that Julia was in fact dancing naked in dockland. I was all for rushing off to Liverpool, but Uncle Simon's practice stopped me. The surgeries were crowded and more people than ever rang up asking me to see their pets. Thanks to misguided kindness and all that Christmas goodwill the animals had overeaten as much as their owners, with the worst possible effects on digestions, bedspreads and carpets.

The goodwill business had misfired all round; there was no trace of Julia.

CHAPTER FIVE

Claire invited me for grilled chops and fried chops and chops in onion-sauce, served each time with all her sympathy; with Tiger's sympathy as well after she'd somehow made him understand that my depression was due to Julia's desertion, that – oddly enough – some men found it hard to do without their girls.

Sometimes their sympathy made me feel Julia had treated me shabbily, sometimes it made me sorry for myself; but at all times Claire's lilac and mustard striped walls and the black ceiling, the paper-pheasants and the siamese cats helped to remind me that *I* was not a Coca-Cola puritan. However slight, that was a consolation. If ever Julia turned up again I wouldn't be plagued by inhibitions; I'd enjoy her to the limits of her sybaritic nature.

One day, when Julia's father had once again told me over the phone that his daughter liked her new appointment but still hadn't given him an address, Claire received me with the kind of face my mother had put on for birthday surprises.

'Michael, we've thought of something!'

I immediately jumped to conclusions. Claire had felt pretty guilty about her part in Julia's desertion; perhaps she'd now discover a means of tracking her down *without* mobilising a squad of detectives.

Claire sparkled with joy. 'I'm sure it'll be just the thing for you.' She looked so pretty that Tiger forgot the chops under the grill.

The three of us rushed to put out the flames.

'Uneatable!' observed Tiger, disconsolately.

'Never mind,' said Claire. 'I've got another packet in the

fridge – I'm going to tell him *now*. Michael, you're coming with me to the first night of Tiger's play!'

If she had turned a hosepipe on me I couldn't have felt more shocked. I went hot and cold in turns – disappointed, angry, touched; especially touched, when it occurred to me that Claire was offering me a share in what was to her a momentous personal experience.

'That's splendid,' I managed to say, hoping it sounded sincere.

'When one's miserable one needs something to look forward to,' Claire told me. 'You see, Tiger, I *knew* he'd be thrilled.'

The Wellington Theatre was foaming with stiff petticoats, rubbing against the solid worth of 'black tie'. One didn't have to *see* the show, said a man with a black beard, it was obvious already that *Three Brassieres to Bond Street* would be a runaway success. (Black-beard, Molly Hooper whispered in my ear, was *the* critic.) The Duke of Alanspring was naïve enough to ask why. *The* critic, looking upon his Grace with contempt, decided to be forbearing; the play, he said, was a 'natural'. One only had to look at *who* had come to see it; one only had to remember the author's age – twenty-two. In fact, he declared, he wouldn't stay; he'd look in on another first night or two.

Claire, far from being offended, was delighted with *the* critic's reaction. Floating along in lilac chiffon, her blonde hair polished to the sheen of Swedish silver, she carried me off to her box. There she unpacked her huge velvet carpet-bag, extracted Chou-en-Lai and Mao-tse-Tung and draped them over her shoulders. The Duke and Winky, John and Molly Hooper draped themselves along the chairs behind her, while I waited apprehensively for the play to begin.

'Absolutely divine,' said the slinky fifty-year-old who

represented the journal *Lady about Town*. 'My dear Miss Brown-Claremont, your cats! A touch of genius. My readers will be fascinated. Do tell me, did you buy the cats to match your dress? Your veterinary surgeon! How charming! My readers will love this – this consideration for your animals.'

'Miss Claremont!' A young reporter with a press-camera pushed his way more firmly into our box. 'You work with the author, don't you?'

'Only as an interior decorator – you know he has an antique shop in Chelsea – the play is entirely his own work.'

'Yes, but knowing the author so well, I thought – perhaps you could tell us something more about the play – the significance of the three brassieres for instance.'

'Tiger believes in the importance of a wholesome sex-life.' Claire nervously clutched Chou-en-Lai.

'Brilliant,' said the reporter. 'Of course, I personally feel the play's absolutely fantastic – the wonderful symbolism – it all makes people appear as stupid as they *are*, as empty, enmeshed in false values. Of course, the author is more subtle.'

Claire gave him a warm smile. 'You must be an author yourself. You understand so well –'

'Well, I'm only a journalist, but I have been working on a play off and on.'

'You must meet Tiger. It's been a hectic night for him, but there'll be a party back-stage – come along, everyone.'

Flashlights blinded us in the box and all the way to the stage. The cats began to cry; I had to put them into Claire's carpet-portmanteau and keep a tight grip on the bag.

Back-stage actors and reporters, Tiger and Claire set about emptying crates of Coca-Cola. For me Claire had thoughtfully provided bottles of whisky, and Tiger was pouring it out by the tumblerful. The only receptacle for its disposal was a pot of geraniums. I had no choice; *one* of us had to get sick. After an hour or so I managed to push the geraniums behind Mrs Miller's pile of broken jam jars – and not too soon; the whisky was beginning to dribble from the hole at the bottom of the pot across the set.

I succeeded in slipping the tumbler into the bag of cats and grabbed a Coca-Cola.

'Good party?' asked Muriel, at breakfast.

'No meat and all bone,' I told her, 'like a certain kind of chop.'

She looked at me attentively. 'You've had too many late nights one way or another.'

'Not with Julia.'

'*This* doesn't look exactly dull,' she said, handing me her morning paper.

The gossip-page was headlined HER CATS AND HER VET ATTEND THREE BRASSIERES; beneath was a picture of Claire and myself grinning at one another like Chou-en-Lai and Mao-tse-Tung. And below that was the usual paragraph of insinuations; was Miss Claire Brown-Claremont, daughter of the millionaire banker, preparing a surprise for her parents (now spending the winter on the yacht of a millionaire shipowner)? Will they come home to a surprise marriage of Claire with one of the young men who have been escorting her – for instance to the first night of Tiger St George Clemens's play?

'Look, Muriel,' I said, furiously, 'this is rubbish. Claire's not interested in any man other than Tiger, and Tiger's too dense to be interested in anything more emotional than theories – about a wholesome sex-life.'

'Sorry, Michael.' Muriel took back the paper but did not resume reading. 'Well, I hope Tiger will get over his theories – though with some men it takes a long time.'

I had never considered that Tiger and my Uncle Simon had anything in common. Yet, I knew Muriel was right. I only wished I had her patience, or Claire's.

At lunchtime I received an envelope containing a news-paper cutting. HER CATS AND HER VET ATTEND THREE BRAS-SIERES . . . looked even worse stripped of the surrounding gossip about other first-nighters. The envelope bore a London postmark. Julia, no matter what her father said, *was* somewhere in London. Only she would have sent me this cutting without comment.

Though I once again drew blanks with phone calls to Baker Street and to the *Purple Pigeon* I felt almost happy. One thing was certain, if Julia did not love me she wouldn't have been stung by the gossip, nor would she have sent the cutting, letting me know how furious she was.

The effect of Julia's envelope was that I became more restless than ever. I had to do *something* non-routine and when Muriel, always tender-hearted and understanding, suggested I should spend the week-end getting to know Lady Jane's horses it seemed a solution of sorts. Though I had a shrewd idea of the amount the Silver Ghost would swallow, I looked forward to driving her full out fifty miles to Hazelbridge.

Hazelbridge was, as the Duke had said, a 'jolly nice place.'

'Fifteenth century,' young Molly Hooper told me. 'There are tons of filth inside these walls. Last year we had to have a new roof put on, and one of the tilers said it was the dirtiest old house he'd ever seen.'

Sir Oliver Hooper, she said, just used the house occasionally for 'working on papers' brought down from his City office; Lady Jane used it because it was beside the stables, John to accommodate friends such as Winky and Tiger who had no country-place, and Molly because she was too young to object to living wherever she was put.

The Duke had his own cottage in the grounds, even older than Hazelbridge House, a former farm-labourer's home where the dirt of ages not only filled the empty spaces behind the walls but lay undisturbed on beams and floor-boards, brick fireplaces, and on the canopies of four-poster beds which had been thrown out of Lady Jane's house and hauled in through the top windows of the Duke's cottage.

But it was not sharp-smelling black London grime; it was earthy dirt, and the slush of the paths and the mud of the paddock were clean dirt, too.

Despite the mud the greyhound gave an impressive performance. Weighing half a stone less than at our first meeting Grey Rainbow chased Masters, on a borrowed motor-bike, with such tenacity and enthusiasm that I could not see why he shouldn't do even better running after a hare on a smooth track. Perhaps his Grace wasn't so eccentric after all in believing Grey Rainbow was a 'solid' investment.

After the dog-trials on Saturday morning I spent the rest of the day examining Lady Jane's horses. Hunters and ponies were in good shape except that lack of exercise had made them somewhat frisky.

On Sunday morning we went out riding, Lady Jane and I on the hunters, Molly – rather sulkily – on Rustler, the largest of the ponies.

'Ponies,' grumbled Molly, trotting beside me. 'I think it's silly keeping them, don't you? I was mad about them when I was small, but it was just a phase. I think people who're mad about horses aren't quite in orbit. I mean – horses are quite nice to look at – but why must Mummy spend thirty pounds a week on six of them? She should send me to university instead – then I'd be a real investment.'

Lady Jane came cantering up. 'Mr Morton, I was thinking of entering Rustler for the Horse of the Year Show. What's your opinion?'

'He looks a first-rate pony in his own class, but he'd need a good deal of training between now and the Show.'

'Oh, of course – I'd like you to see him jump. There are

some fences in the Claremonts' paddock. Molly, we'll take him over this afternoon.'

'Oh, Mummy! Must I!'

'What's the matter with you, child? You're getting thoroughly lazy – if you like you can ring Angela and Patricia. It's a lovely day for jumping; they'll come.'

'The ground's slippery,' muttered Molly.

'Nonsense.'

The ground *was* still wet, but the sun was warm for late February and I thought conditions would improve by the afternoon.

We skirted a paw of the South Downs and turned into a lane between fields. Already the buds on the whitethorn were swelling and I saw a crocus ready to unfurl. The air carried a moist scent of sap. I thought of Julia. I thought she'd like riding with me through these lanes heavy with spring.

Angela's and Patricia's pride in their ponies did not improve Molly's enthusiasm for taking Rustler over the fences. She sat and watched her friends jump, muttering an occasional 'well done' which was no more than the conditioned reflex of someone who had attended countless horse-shows and gymkhanas.

'Molly, pull yourself together,' said Lady Jane. 'You're being childish. If those plays you see in London are having a bad effect on you I won't allow John to take you in future.'

'It's nothing to do with the plays, Mummy.'

'What else? Whenever you've been staying in town you come home feeling silly and sluggish.'

'Don't fuss, Mummy.' Molly dug her heels in Rustler, and galloped off.

In her bad temper she took Rustler over the fences much faster than Angela or Patricia, achieving the nearest thing to a Spanish style I had seen from a girl of fifteen. There was no doubt that Molly was a beautiful rider and I could see reasons for Lady Jane's ambitions.

'Rustler's action is good, isn't it,' she said, happily.

'Excellent.'

'Molly should make him pick up his feet a bit more. I know he can do it. Molly!'

'Yes, Mummy?'

'Well done . . . Now, let's put up fence one and two.'

I dismounted and gave them a hand. Molly seemed to have overcome her earlier reluctance.

When, at her first attempt over the higher fences, Rustler knocked down a bar she told Angela to put it back, and returned to fence one. Rustler sailed over and approached fence two with confidence.

His front legs were well up to the level of the fence when he suddenly seemed to slip sideways. He bucked violently, threw Molly over the fence and himself heavily crashed down on the jumping-off side. Lady Jane got to them faster than I did.

'Quiet, Rusty, quiet.' She patted the neck of the trembling pony. 'Mr Morton – his stifle-joint!' She was breathless with agitation. 'Is his stifle all right? If he's lamed himself –'

I was examining Molly, who was lying still, white and unconscious.

'Mr Morton!' Lady Jane called, impatiently. 'Rusty's had a nasty fall – I don't want him to move before you've looked at that joint.'

Angela and Patricia had congregated round the pony. Molly was still lying motionless. I did not think she'd broken a limb, but she might have suffered a head injury; at least there was bound to be concussion.

'Don't worry about Molly.' Lady Jane sounded somewhat exasperated. 'She'll be all right. *I* often passed out when I was thrown; don't think she's broken anything – isn't Rusty's joint swelling up?'

I looked at Rustler's stifle-joint, which appeared to be

precisely where it was meant to be, and I kept looking at Molly who was slowly sitting up, somewhat dazed.

'All right, Moll?' asked Angela.

'Yes,' said Molly, in a small voice. She got to her feet, staggering. 'I've got a headache.'

'Up you go.' Lady Jane held Rustler, while Molly mounted rather clumsily. 'I'll give you an aspirin when we get home.'

'I feel sick, Mummy.'

'Don't worry, you'll be all right – Rusty's all right, isn't that lucky.'

'Yes, isn't it!' echoed Angela and Patricia.

'I've been lucky,' said Masters. 'Got him at last.' His statement was as incongruous as his cortège, which I'd met on my way to the Duke's cottage. Avoiding the mud of the fields I had taken the long road through the village; Masters had caught me up in the High Street. Wearing army surplus trousers and battle-dress he'd trundled up a bicycle with the best part of a tree trailing behind what looked like a couple of pram-wheels. Behind the tree Grey Rainbow was leaping about as if guarding a quarry that might attempt a getaway.

'Got him at last,' mused Masters, with obvious satisfaction. 'I've been watching him these past twelve months. He was a tough one right enough.' It seemed to me Masters' whole personality had changed. Having developed a distinctive Sussex burr he no longer even sounded like the Duke's gentleman. 'I kept an eye on him.'

'On whom?' I asked.

'The wind's bound to bring him down, I said to myself,' continued Masters. 'And to be sure – last night I heard him. Mind you, Mr Morton, when I got over this afternoon he was still hanging on, but not so as you could say I cut him down.'

It suddenly dawned on me who Masters' lethal enemy

83

was. 'You mean that tree?'

Masters glanced over his shoulder at the trailing trunk. 'Half a tree,' he corrected me. 'He was the toughest one I ever got. You'd have thought the gale in January would bring him down – but no, not him. There he was, hanging on like a young one.'

'Where did you get – him?' I asked.

'In the park.'

'The park?'

'That's the trouble, sir, the park – and the original manor – they've been taken over by the National Trust. It's a shame us not being allowed to cut down trees, seeing it was his Grace's property – all of it. Mind you, sir, his Grace couldn't afford to keep it up, and it wasn't his fault either – horses,' he added as if he disliked them even more than the Duke did. 'Horses; that's where the Alanspring money went. We'd have *nothing* left if it weren't for Sir Oliver Hooper; he bought the new manor for Lady Jane.

'Lady Jane,' Masters chuckled. It seemed the victory over the dead tree, or perhaps the National Trust, had so excited him that he couldn't stop talking. 'She met Sir Oliver at Claridges, when her great-aunt was ill. The old lady used to live there, and Lady Jane called on her every morning. If her great-aunt wasn't awake she'd wait in the lounge where Sir Oliver was reading his morning paper. Well – in the end he *had* to marry her.'

'I see,' I said, noncommittally.

'It stands to reason, Mr Morton, doesn't it? If he'd asked a waiter to bring her a paper it would have been rude. And he couldn't *buy* a paper for a perfect stranger, could he? Awkward, that's what it was for Sir Oliver. I *know* because I myself can't stand it either when someone's trying to read my paper over my shoulder.'

We turned off the High Street into the path skirting the Hoopers' grounds. Grey Rainbow, a hundred yards from his owner's cottage, arched his back and sprinted ahead.

'He's in fine form,' said Masters, proudly, 'a bit thin, but fit. His Grace is pleased.'

'We'll soon have him running races.'

'Oh, no, Mr Morton. Rainbow won't go on a track.'

'Look here, Masters, is there anything I don't yet know about this dog?'

'He's a good dog,' said Masters, evasively.

'He's perfectly healthy.'

'Yes, sir.'

'Then why shouldn't he do well on a race-track?'

'Well, sir, Rainbow's a funny one – I mean, some people are funny too, aren't they? What he needs now is a good warm bath. I hope his Grace has got the water ready.'

The Duke stood in his kitchen, his head almost touching the worm-holed timbers which an estate-agent would have described as 'a wealth of old oak beams'. Wearing a pair of thick motoring-gloves he was stirring a huge frying-pan full of unrecognisable food. The old double-burner oil-cooker was dangerously tilted sideways where an iron pot of water was simmering away, adding steam to the choking oil-fumes.

'*Surprise d'Alanspring* for dinner,' the Duke greeted us.

'His Grace's own invention,' said Masters.

'If I didn't know he hates cooking,' said the Duke, 'I'd flatter myself it's his favourite dish. Masters, it's not quite ready, so you can bath Rainbow first. I've put his bowl in front of the fire.'

Though the table was laid for dinner the one and only living-room looked like a place permanently geared to the needs of a young baby. On a mat in front of the fire stood a zinc bath, beside it a stool with soap, sponge and brushes, while the chairs were cluttered up with towels and blankets.

Grey Rainbow liked his bath; he liked it so much that he was dancing in the water, splashing and shaking himself until the dinner-table was doused in drops and dollops of foam. While I rubbed him down with a warmed towel Masters took away the bath and wiped the hearth, but not the dinner-plates.

The Duke came in from the kitchen, still wearing his gauntlets. 'Are we ready? Masters, there's a bottle of the Friedenau Riesling in the hay-box. You can serve now.' He regarded his damp greyhound with satisfaction. 'Well, Morton, ever seen a finer hound?' He stripped off his gloves and playfully threw them to the dog. 'Up Rainbow! Pick 'em up, boy!'

Rainbow responded with a pitiful howl. He cowered into the soggy towels on the floor, hiding his face, began to shiver, and presently sneezed once, twice, half a dozen times. It seemed incredible that so frisky and healthy a dog should be reduced – within seconds – to this wretched bundle of fur and bones.

'Masters!' shouted the Duke. 'What have you done to the dog? You've let him catch cold!'

'No, your Grace, he's a bit excited, that's all.' He picked up the Duke's gloves and put them in a drawer of the Dutch dresser. 'It's only the bath, your Grace.'

'But the dog *likes* his bath.'

'Yes, that's why he gets a bit over-excited.'

'Morton, is that right?'

It seemed to be. Rainbow's fit of shivering and sneezing had stopped as suddenly as it began. The dog was perfectly calm, his nose was cold, and he contentedly stretched out in front of the fire. But I was still puzzled. It was the first time I'd seen the slightest trace of hysteria in Rainbow, and it made me wonder whether he had suffered similar attacks in the past. The Duke said he hadn't; Masters, I thought, would not tell me if he had. Masters, apparently, had made up his mind that Rainbow was 'a funny one', as 'funny as some *people* are'. Whether that was Masters' general opinion or a carefully formed conclusion remained to be seen, I felt sure I wouldn't find out by questioning Masters.

'I'll take another look at him when we're back in town,' I told the Duke. 'Just to see what the week-end in the country's done for him.'

'Think you should?'

'It'll be a social call,' I said, rashly waiving my fees.

'Very good of you, Morton.' The Duke passed me the bowl of *surprise*. 'Help yourself – of course, I know you're *interested* in Rainbow. He isn't a run-of-the-mill animal like a horse.'

'No animal is run-of-the-mill,' I told him. 'Each animal has as distinctive a character as a person.' I went on to prove my point, maybe because Masters had opened the third bottle of wine, maybe because the intimacy of the little cottage and the warmth of the log-fire made me remember another kind of warmth.

I told the Duke of Miss Shaw's tough little mongrel, of the psychiatrist's fox, of Mrs Topper's poodle who wanted a four-legged bitch, and of the cobra which came to me like a dog when I whistled 'On Ilkley Moor baht 'at.' A part of me, the one that usually resisted alcohol-animation, knew that all those animal stories trotted out for my host's entertainment were in fact trotted out for my own benefit; the next best thing to being with Julia was talking and thinking of her.

'A girl with a big snake can't disappear,' said the Duke, 'not if the snake is – in a sense – her profession. If she's not in a cabaret she must be in a circus.'

When I called at Tiger's shop on my way home he and Claire agreed that the Duke's idea was brilliant. Where could a performing snake be if not in a circus? And it was a more likely place than a cabaret. They offered to visit Billy Smart's circus the same night; it was the only one in London at the time. If we drew a blank we'd think again; for instance how to check circuses in other parts of the country.

'I asked Mr Topper whether he'd heard from Julia,' Claire told me. 'He was here last Friday – he said he hardly remembered Julia. What's odd is that he didn't forget about the cat-pictures. He wanted to buy paintings like the ones we gave you.'

'There were no Chinese pictures left,' said Tiger. 'But he bought a folder of Victorian etchings of cats.'

Claire laughed. 'Do you know what else? The most ghastly Victorian dresser, with masses of pussies carved all over the doors and drawers.'

'I advised him against it.' Tiger sounded unhappy. 'The dresser was part of a lot I bought at an auction. I put it in the basement and forgot about it – if Topper hadn't insisted on going down –'

'Well, he did,' said Claire. 'And you only charged him ten pounds. The wood was worth as much – the thing is, what would Topper want with all these cats?'

'His wife doesn't like cats.'

'People *are* impossible,' said Claire, with feeling. 'If I had a husband –' she broke off and blushed to the roots of her Swedish-silver hair. 'Well, Michael, try not to worry. We'll ring you whether we find Julia or not.'

I think I had a presentiment that Claire and Tiger wouldn't find Julia. At least I was not surprised when they didn't. Yet it was Claire who gave me news of Julia at last, and it was not of a kind that gave me peace of mind. It was a half page from a newspaper, the sexiest Sunday.

There was a picture of Julia in a shiny, slinky dress, her black hair piled up into a pagoda, her eyes bright with amusement, laughing at her serpent who appeared to be chasing an astonishing number of well-dressed people. It was a picture of chaos; upturned chairs, a debris of broken plates and glasses on the floor, a waiter with hands lifted in supplication, a man diving between a flurry of women.

'Chaos at the Dernier Cri Restaurant,' I read. 'When an attractive, dark girl arrived at the Dernier Cri with her man-about-town escort none of the other guests realised that the unusual trimming of her gold sheath dress was a live cobra. Nor did this startling fact become obvious while Miss Julia Hanley and Captain Franks were enjoying oysters, a tournedos steak, and délice maison.

'Cobby, the serpent, was patient. But when her mistress and Captain Franks engaged in a long, deep conversation over coffee and liqueurs, Cobby got bored. She slowly slipped from Miss Hanley's neck to the floor and made her way beneath the tables on to the lap of model-girl Anthea Arlett.

'The terrified screams of Miss Arlett and a glass of wine spilled over the cobra by her friend Claud Delsey so alarmed the reptile that it shot away in search of a calmer resting-place. Alas, there were no accommodating laps. While Miss Hanley and Captain Franks looked on with somewhat cruel amusement all customers fled, some without paying their bills.

'Said Captain Franks: "The management were naturally a bit upset but I gave them a cheque covering the unpaid bills, and we parted good friends."

'Said Miss Hanley: "I can't understand why people should make such a fuss about a cobra in a restaurant. After all, people take dogs. Recently some woman even took a couple of siamese cats to the theatre. Cobras aren't nearly so much nuisance – they don't make a noise. Why I took Cobby out dining? Well, she hates being left alone. And Sidney didn't mind her coming with us. Actually, he's rather fond of Cobby. I think other people would be if they got to know snakes. Cobras are marvellous pets. I *know*, I've lived with them all my life." '

Perhaps serpents were the only creatures Julia was fit to live with, I told Muriel. Perhaps the ubiquitous Captain Franks was a snake, too. So Julia and Sidney Franks were engaged in a long deep conversation, were they! The Captain was fond of Cobby, was he!

'This won't get you anywhere,' said Muriel, sensibly.

'Don't know that I have anywhere to get.'

'Nonsense, you want her back, don't you?'

'Yes,' I admitted, 'if this fellow Franks –'

'Well, I think she's been using him to annoy *you*,' declared Muriel. 'Why do you think she bothered sending you the cutting of Claire and yourself at the theatre? Because she hates you? Because she's vicious?'

'No, Julia isn't vicious – she's got a temper –'

'You hurt her, Michael, even if you didn't mean to. Still,' she picked up the scrap of newspaper, 'this will be a help.'

'Glad you think so.'

'Pull yourself together – at least you know she's still in London.'

CHAPTER SIX

Julia's father, in his mild vague way, confirmed that she was again living in London and my telephone call to Leamington Spa at last resulted in his giving me her address. Only it wasn't her address; the c/o turned out to be a dancer's chiropody establishment where Julia occasionally dropped in for a pedicure and to pick up her letters.

The pugilists at the *Purple Pigeon* knew even less, but Bill eventually let slip that Captain Franks still spent the odd evening in the bar.

I rejected the idea of working my way through the Franks in the telephone book. If I did get the right one on the line what would I say to him? Presumably Julia had gone out to dinner with him of her own free will. And was he likely, especially if she'd become his girl friend, to give me her address?

Diplomacy was the thing; meet the fellow, have a few drinks with him, talk about animals in general and snakes in particular. I could just hear him: 'Funny you should mention it; I happen to have a friend who has a cobra and if you whistle "On Ilkley Moor baht 'at" that snake comes to you like a dog.' What was I going to say then? 'How incredible! I must say I'd like to meet that snake.'

Muriel, always down to earth, told me to stop worrying. I'd think of the right approach after meeting the Captain.

For the next ten days I hung about the *Purple Pigeon*, sometimes adding my frustrations to the frustrations of the other men in the audience, sometimes spinning out a couple of beers in the bar. No Captain Franks; so there was nothing to do but compare the shape of Maisie's breasts with

91

Florry's, the size and elevation of Mimi's nipples with June's. Since the *Purple Pigeon* was beer *and* breasts or nothing, my nightly trips to Soho – counting the Silver Ghost's fodder – became something of a financial strain as well as a nightmare of the flesh.

One night, after I had again stared unseeingly at the sexless 'artistic' flesh to the accompaniment of 'In a Monastery Garden,' Bill – the more sympathetic of the pugilists – tapped me on the shoulder.

'Captain Franks's in the bar.'

Out of my depth, I gave him a 50p.

'Thanks, gov'ner. Over there – by hisself, talking to Annie.'

I don't know why I had imagined Franks as a middle-aged ex-supplies officer with an alcohol-flush complexion, bleary pale eyes and a developing paunch covered by a tailor-made drape. He was nothing of the kind. The tailoring – somewhat too fashionable Italian drape Irish tweed – was all I'd expected but the man inside the suit was tall, lean, sandy, with a St Moritz tan. I noticed he had a thick growth of hair on the backs of his hands, the mark – as a female vet-student had once informed me – of a man who is good in bed.

I went up to the bar and asked Annie for a half-pint of bitter. Franks was drinking something short, probably Scotch.

'Haven't we met before?' I couldn't think of anything less corny, but in the circumstances it seemed all right. After all, the idea was not to alarm the fellow.

'May have done,' he lied, amiably. 'Maybe here.'

'I used to look after a patient upstairs – a snake.'

'Morton!' he exclaimed, clapping his hairy hands on my shoulders. 'Now, *there's* a coincidence! I was going to ring you. Julia told me what a good vet you are. I think a man who can cure a snake's bound to be able to deal with horses. Do you?'

92

'Of course.' The conversation was not going as I wanted. 'Julia's snake's most unusual, isn't she? I remember the first time I saw Cobby –'

'Well, that's settled then. You'll look after our horses. Look here, let's talk in comfort. Come to my flat – hello, Jake!' A tight-trousered youth with a crew-cut had come in. 'Hang on a moment, Morton, will you?' Franks joined the youth who had produced what looked like a farmer's stock-list. Only, the youth didn't look like a farmer's boy.

Out of his grubby jersey he produced more papers and a pencil, which he gave to Franks. They did some fast talking.

'Not Oberon,' I heard Franks say. 'Use your loaf, son . . . the French filly. Take a chance on her . . . Don't tell me it's out. All right . . . tell Williams I sent you.'

Was the man a tipster? He didn't look like one. All I wanted from him was Julia's address, yet I became curious about his connection with horses.

'Sorry, Morton!' he called. 'Be with you in a tick.'

'Julia?' Franks poured me another whisky. 'No idea where she hangs out.' He said it so casually that I believed him.

'How do you get in touch with her?'

'I don't. She rang me up once or twice, so I took her to dinner. I like her snake.'

'Her snake?' I asked, rather foolishly.

'Funny creature, isn't it?'

'And Julia?'

'Well, I'm not a woman's man – you understand. Julia's better than most. She doesn't expect anything. We eat, talk, but once out of the restaurant she gets in a taxi and takes herself home.'

'And you have no clue where *home* is?'

'None whatever. Look here; your name's Michael, isn't it? Julia's been a bit hard on you. At least, that's what it seems like to me. She's been talking about you; I know the course

93

of true lust hasn't been running smoothly. But if I were you I shouldn't worry. She'll come round.'

'That's what *I* said – several months ago.' The last thing I'd expected was Sidney Franks's sympathy, the sympathy of a queer.

'That's my opinion,' he said. 'You've hurt her pride, Michael. But she'll forget all about it when celibacy becomes a bit much for her. She's no fish – oh, I don't know that from crude experience. But people like me understand women far better than fellows who need them. We get our sex the hard way. Take my advice; give her time for finding an excuse to come to *you*. And now let's get down to business. We can talk while we eat.'

Sidney Franks went out and I presently heard him run water in his bathroom. Fishtail Mansions seemed an odd place for a countryman. It was comfortable and hot but I couldn't lose for a moment the feeling of being hedged in by hundreds of similar flats all crammed with people, all crammed with problems, at least fifty per cent of them living with unread books draped round a phoney brick fireplace, with a large-screen TV set, and a well-stocked cocktail cabinet. And all the time the tenants not yet clubbed down by the sheer size of the place would sit in their padded cages conscious of the proximity of those in the padded cages on the left and the right, above and below.

'Want a wash?' asked Franks. 'No? Right, let's go.'

We went down in the lift, down a passage like a primeval jungle-track, only instead of branches and creepers there was a forest of pipes, electric cables and switch-boxes. Some mist off the streets had seeped in and it seemed to me we were walking through a steaming bog. Suddenly, at the end of the passage, I was blinded by a cobalt technicolour light.

It turned out to be a swimming-pool, and round the swimming-pool – like fish out of water, literally – sat sleek people, in sleek clothes, eating sleek English dinners with

94

French names.

Of course, Sidney – by then I was calling him Sidney – had established Christian-name intimacy with the waiters. Johnny, with an I-know-your-tastes-air, recommended the snails and Raymond a carafe of Portuguese Vila Real; so much better than a bottle for people with 'a taste in wines.'

Sidney told me what 'the score' was. The horses which would be in my care were the last of the famous Skeffington string. They belonged to Miss Augusta, the only surviving member of the industrialist's family. Sidney Franks's father had been old man Skeffington's trainer, one of the most successful in the country. When he died, two years earlier, Sidney had left the Army and taken over the five remaining horses. They were now stabled at Miss Skeffington's residence of Craftley Manor, Surrey.

Miss Skeffington had sold most of her horses to America, chiefly to raise money towards paying the death duty on her father's estate. Recently the debts had been paid off and Miss Skeffington intended breeding new stock from her mare Sheba and the famous stallion Oberon the Second. Those two race-horses, plus the fillies Winsome and Cybele and the colt Septimus, were in Sidney's opinion an excellent nucleus for reviving what had been one of the greatest stables in the country.

It sounded an exciting proposition. Miss Skeffington would be an important addition to the new owners I had to collect if I was to achieve a partnership in Uncle Simon's practice. But there was one possible snag.

'Surely Miss Skeffington already has a vet,' I suggested. 'I should have thought a vet who specialises in horses.'

'That's the trouble,' said Sidney. 'Until we sold most of the stud to America Mr Brogan looked after our horses –'

'Phil Brogan?'

'Yes. You know him?'

95

'He was in my year at the College.'

'I see.' Sidney did not sound too pleased. 'Nice fellow. But – frankly – over-ambitious in my opinion. Five horses, no matter how good, are nothing to him. When he came to Craftley he was after the big owners – the Roger Blandings. Got them, too. In a sense they're our rivals – though of course we're friendly. Yesterday, before I went up to town, I had a word with Phil Brogan. He's quite a decent sort. He said if we felt we wanted a change of vets it would be all right with him. Is that good enough for you?'

It was good enough for me to go down to Craftley in the Silver Ghost. Sidney Franks had offered me a lift in his Alfa Romeo, but I wanted a word with Phil Brogan without giving Sidney the impression that I was checking up on his story.

Phil, whom I remembered as a cheerful raw-boned student, had turned into a large confidence-inspiring professional man, nicely settled in a chaotic-looking farm run by his weather-beaten, jolly wife, Fiona.

Without being asked the elderly maid who had shown me into the dining-room produced some bottles of beer, which Fiona served in pewter tankards.

'I'm glad you're going to look after Miss Skeff's horses,' said Phil.

'Why?' I asked him, wondering why he wasn't doing it himself.

Phil laughed. 'Because she's an old sweety, and I feel sorry for her. All right, no need to ask. All her life – and she's in her seventies now – *someone* always looked after her – a butler, a housekeeper, maids, her father. Gradually all the old family retainers died off and then, three or four years ago, her father died. He must have been ninety-five or more. Well, it was late in the day for her to learn how to run a house, let alone stables.'

96

'Stables? I thought Sidney Franks was doing that for her.'

'He is, when he isn't in London. I'm not saying he doesn't understand horses.'

'But?'

'I don't know,' Phil shrugged his shoulders. 'I don't much care for Sidney. That's why I don't particularly want Miss Skeff's horses on my panel – provided they're in safe hands. Come over to the surgery; I'll give you my notes.'

According to Phil Brogan's observations Miss Skeffington's remaining horses were of the highest quslity. No unsoundness in any of the animals, except that Oberon the Second had once been found to have lice below the mane and on the withers, a thing that can happen to the most aristocratic animal.

'Sheba's true to her name.' Phil turned up a page of his notes. 'The way she flashes her clitoris makes me suspicious. She may be a nymphomaniac. Certainly when she's in oestrus poor Oberon doesn't get much peace – she expects him to serve her every time they meet – I'd say, keep an eye on Sheba in mid-winter; if she hasn't calmed down take another look at her ovaries. I haven't worried unduly because, after all, Sheba and Oberon have produced a fine colt and a nice filly. Deliveries were normal. Maybe Sheba's a sexy mare out of excessive maternal feeling.'

'Has Miss Skeffington raced any of these horses?'

'Septimus and Cybele have been on the course last season – what I can't understand is why they weren't even placed. They should have been.'

'What do you think happened?'

'Impossible to guess. Maybe their training was inadequate.'

'Phil, you're handing over to me because you don't get on too well with Sidney Franks?'

'It's mutual. We agreed on the change of vets. I'm glad he's chosen you – and if there's anything I can do, any time, let me know. Join us for lunch?'

'I think I should get along to Miss Skeffington's. I'll just say good-bye to Fiona.'

In the dining-room the table was laid. In the centre stood a large bowl of mixed salad and a dish of sliced cold meat-loaf. While Fiona was saying she hoped I'd drop in again a tough-looking farm-cat had climbed on a chair and pulled a slice of the meat-loaf on to the floor.

'Tabby!' Fiona grabbed the slice. 'Naughty cat!' With her left hand she managed to wallop the fleeing Tabby, with her right she dexterously re-fitted Tabby's slice to the rest of the meat-loaf. 'Michael, are you sure you won't stay for lunch?'

'Quite sure, thank you.' I hoped it didn't sound as if I'd turned down her hospitality for fear of food-poisoning.

'You poor man!' exclaimed Miss Skeffington. 'No lunch after your long journey. You must have something to eat before you see the horses; I insist.' She glanced about her kitchen, her pretty old-lady's face eager and bewildered. Her blue eyes travelled along the cobweb-hung walls, over a kitchen table piled high with stale bread, bits of butter in paper, empty sardine tins and stacks of newspapers. She discovered what she wanted, a large modern record-player piled high with unopened tins of sardines.

'I know,' she said, with a serene smile. 'Sardines! – so good for the voice. I hope you won't mind if I don't keep you company, but I have lunched.' From the dim corner beside the gas-cooker she produced a card-table which she spread with a crumpled cloth. 'Would you open the tin, Mr Morton? I think men are much cleverer at that kind of thing.'

I helped tip the sardines on a beautiful but badly cracked Spode china plate, and Miss Skeffington arranged stained but crested cutlery either side of it. She found a few slices of almost fresh bread and a piece of butter.

'You should have something to drink.' Painfully her heavy rheumatic body dragged itself to the larder and back. She held up a bottle of champagne for my inspection. 'Would this be suitable, Mr Morton? My dear father kept a very good cellar, but I'm afraid I don't know much about wines.'

'I think you should keep the champagne, Miss Skeffington. Keep it for a special occasion.'

'Oh, but this is a special occasion. I don't entertain a new veterinary surgeon every day.'

'You are very kind, but I would actually prefer a glass of water.'

'*I* know, I shall make tea. Would you like lapsang?'

'Very much.'

'How nice. Then I'll join you.'

When we sat opposite one another, each with a paper-thin cracked Chinese porcelain cup in hand, Miss Skeffington began to discuss the news. The Prime Minister, she thought, was a splendid man for the job, so calm and sure of himself; we were fortunate in having someone who was not afraid of those difficult Russians. 'And did you see, Mr Morton, there was an article in the *Daily Telegraph* about some new missile. But I did not quite understand how it's meant to work.'

'The Firestreak? I believe it can be fired from U.S.A.2, the American artificial satellite.'

'How interesting!' Miss Skeffington took a sip of tea. 'Well, Mr Morton, I have quite made up my mind about the Firestreak. I shall *not* take any notice of it.'

I wished 'those difficult Russians' would dismiss the Firestreak with as much equanimity.

'Of course, this is no reflection on America, Mr Morton. I have the highest regard for that country – especially since I sold some of my dear father's horses to that nice American gentleman – now, what was his name? Mr – Mr Allerton Newtonson – isn't it strange? There are always either too

99

many syllables in American names or not enough – yes, Mr Newtonson was most accommodating. I was quite in favour of selling him the rest of my horses – I feel I'm too old to have the worry of race-horses. But dear Sidney wouldn't let me sell.'

'They're *your* horses, Miss Skeffington.'

'I know, Mr Morton, but I do feel if one is fortunate enough to have expert advice at hand one should take it, don't you agree?'

'Yes – well, if you'll excuse me I'll go to the stables now.'

'Oh, no, you must have a rest after your lunch – so bad for one to rush about immediately after a meal. I'll play you a piece of music.' She got up, hobbled across to the record-player and selected a disc. 'Shall we listen to a song by that young man, Cliff Richard? Cliff? I suppose he's an American.'

Miss Skeffington had adjusted the player to the wrong speed, so that Cliff's voice seemed to emerge from somewhere below a tumbled skyscraper. 'My square's a honey' it growled, and then in a prolonged howl of agony, 'My square's a haoo-haoo-honey.'

Miss Skeffington smiled. 'My dear father used to say I was tone-deaf. But I think in this one thing he may have been mistaken; I'm very fond of music. Of course, I don't understand it as well as he did. He was a great patron of music. Every year, on mid-summer eve, he engaged musicians and a company to play for us the whole of the *Chocolate Soldier* – ah, the young man has finished his song. Now, there is another one I like very much – such a pretty tune, though it *is* foreign as well, "I'm gonna wash that man right outa my hair." '

It was three o'clock before I got to the stables. On an average it takes three-quarters of an hour to examine a horse thoroughly, and I like doing it by daylight. Since I had to return to London the best I could hope for was that I'd be

100

able to form a general impression of the horses' condition.

There was no sign of Sidney Franks but there was a boy ready to assist me, and that boy was Jake, the character with the crew-cut and tight pants who had met Sidney at the *Purple Pigeon*. He still looked like a Soho delinquent, but there was no doubt he was used to handling horses.

I took the horses' temperatures, pulse and respiration rates, observed the jugular pulsation, the respiratory movement of the flanks, and I auscultated their hearts. As usual I introduced myself to each horse with a lump of sugar and later dropped another on the floor to find out if the animal had any trouble in getting its head to the ground.

Finding no unsoundness during the first part of the examination I told Jake to take out the horses one by one. The first one he led out of the stable was Oberon. The stallion's eyes quickly adjusted to the change of light.

Jake held the leading rein close under Oberon's chin, keeping his head high, and immediately began trotting him round the yard.

'Stop!' I shouted. Jake's technique was only too familiar. I didn't like it. It was common practice among shady horse-dealers to 'warm up' a horse in order to disguise lameness. A trotting horse does not show lameness as clearly as a walking animal, nor is lameness so easily spotted after the horse has been made to 'warm up' its joints. The next stage of a shady performance is that the horse's handler, having tired himself in the preliminary trotting, pretends breathlessness and finishes up with a slow walk.

'I told you to *walk* him,' I said, more sharply than I'd intended. 'When I want a trot I'll let you know.'

'Yes, sir,' said Jake, meekly enough.

Yet with each horse he brought out there was a moment when he took the rein close under the chin and *almost* broke into a run. Clearly Jake's habits were well established; and they were habits he wouldn't have acquired under a respectable owner or trainer. However, I thought that was not sufficient reason for distrusting the boy. It was possible he had been instructed to show horses in this particular manner without knowing why. The lad was no more than seventeen or eighteen.

The horses, at any rate, showed no defect of any kind, least of all lameness. Sheba was the most restless for handling, even friskier than the colt.

She danced out of her stable, aware of her great beauty from poll to pastern. Even in the failing light her black coat was gleaming, and when she lifted her head the white blaze shone like the jewel on the forehead of an Indian dancing-girl. She gazed at Oberon's stable, ears up, and made a soft, low neighing sound.

Stealthily, while Jake led her round the yard, she widened the circles until she practically touched Oberon's stable-door. Again the soft call and then, suddenly, her tail went up and she flashed her clitoris, a brazen, touching appeal to the restless stallion inside.

'Whore!' cursed Jake, almost unable to hold her. 'Here! Damned whore!'

I took the rein from him, put myself between Oberon's stable and the mare, and talked to her. 'No good, Sheba. You're a beauty all right. Steady, Sheba, steady! You're not having Oberon now. Whoa! Quiet, girl.'

'Aye, some girl,' said Jake, in a broad Scots accent. 'A whore, and I've seen nae ither like her.' It seemed to me Sheba's performance had shaken him, as much as he admired her eroticism.

'Come on, Sheba,' I coaxed. Gradually, as I played the rein, stroked her neck, and talked, Sheba's tail went down. Once again she neighed, no longer at that provocative excited pitch, and then she accepted my lump of sugar, and quietly enough let me take her into her stable.

I returned to the house, where Miss Skeffington was keeping warm a pot of tea on the hob of the kitchen-fire. I told her how good, I thought, her horses were, which did not seem to interest her greatly, and I told her the Cybele and Septimus should give her a profitable racing season, which interested her even less.

'Dear Sidney will be so pleased,' she said. 'Now, come with me, Mr Morton – this way.' She opened a door that led from the kitchen, through a half-furnished morning-room, into a long stone-flagged passage. 'Will you walk in front of me, please – I prefer it, if you don't mind. My leg is – a little troublesome.'

I realised, with pity and affection, that this old lady with the angelic face was still feminine enough to wish to hide the clumsiness of her rheumatic movements. She had not forgotten her years of beauty, and some of it she'd certainly salvaged for her old age.

She directed me to a suite of rooms on the first floor. A small sitting-room, a library, several bedrooms were crammed with fine antique furniture covered in dust and cobwebs. On some of the pieces I saw the marks of woodworm and death-watch beetle, and the whole floor smelled of mould and decay.

'I'm afraid the house is a little neglected,' said Miss Skeffington. 'I have no resident servant now, and Mrs Wiley – my woman – is often too busy to come. But I have prepared a nice room for you.'

'It's kind of you, Miss Skeffington, but I'm afraid I have to go back to London.'

'Tonight! I think you young people do too much. How long will the journey take you?'

'Only an hour and a half.'

'That must be tiring after a day with horses – but I won't detain you. Perhaps you'll be able to make use of this room another time. I think you'd find it restful.'

'It looks most comfortable,' I assured her. She had

obviously worked very hard at making up a bed and moving the dust from one part of the room to another, but cobwebs, moths and mouse-droppings had defeated her.

'You'll have a cup of tea before you go, won't you?'

In the kitchen the card-table was set; there was even a plate of thin bread and butter.

'Yes, I do believe young people nowadays use their energies a little recklessly.' Miss Skeffington offered me a jar of jam. 'I have said so to Sidney. *He* is so busy travelling to London and – oh, Newmarket, I think. And then he has to attend all those race-meetings.'

I wondered what Miss Skeffington would have made of Sidney's attendances at the *Purple Pigeon* – of the striptease joint itself, run by an elder of the kirk.

'Of course, dear Sidney's so conscientious – always thinking of my interests. He keeps meeting prospective buyers for the horses. I shall *have* to sell them, but Sidney won't let me part with them below a certain price.'

That, as I remembered it, was not Sidney's story. 'What does he advise you to do?' I asked.

'Oh, our plan is to race Septimus and Cybele. Sidney tells me Septimus has every chance of doing well at Ascot this season. And he says Cybele will – how did he put it? – walk away at Goodwood. Sidney expects to meet important buyers at the races.'

'Yes,' I had to admit, 'if your horses won you'd get a higher price for them all, including Sheba and Oberon.'

'I'm glad you agree, Mr Morton – I will be so relieved when my stables are closed down. Horses are expensive and my income . . . Well, my dear father couldn't have foreseen it . . . The pound isn't as valuable as it used to be . . . Your work must be so like a doctor's.' It seemed Miss Skeffington felt somewhat guilty for having disclosed her financial troubles. A reflection on her father's management? There was a pathetic self-consciousness about her sudden change of

104

subject. 'Are you called out at night, Mr Morton?'

'Occasionally.'

'I thought so. I always felt sorry for the doctors – you see, my dear father – he was a strong man, yet any time he felt unwell it was always in the middle of the night – but perhaps animals are more sensible than people?'

'On the whole they are.'

'You will think me foolish, Mr Morton – but do you know what I'd like to do? I'd love to sail to America. All my life I longed to go abroad; perhaps if the horses were sold –'

It was nine o'clock before I left Miss Skeffington's kitchen, having declined a sardine-supper and promised to spend a week-end at Craftley Manor.

As I drove past the big converted barn I heard Cliff Richard's voice from a room above the garage cubicles. At a window, with the light behind them, I saw Jake in a clinch with a girl. On the outskirts of the village, where the road narrowed behind the church, I passed Sidney's Alfa Romeo. I could hardly complain about his absence from the stables which had, after all, allowed me to give Miss Skeffington's horses an unbiased examination, yet Sidney's perfectly timed return made me feel uneasy.

CHAPTER SEVEN

When I saw Sidney Franks again, at my own surgery, he had perfect explanations for everything. He'd kept away from Craftley so that I could form my own opinions of the horses *and* of their owner. He'd known Miss Skeff all his life, he told me, and he loved her like a mother. But there was no doubt she had aged – mentally.

She had always been a little eccentric, but since her father's death she had 'let herself go'. There was no need for a woman of her means to exist on sardines and tea or to let the house fall about her ears while she lived in kitchen-squalor. The saddest thing of all was that she was incapable of making up her mind on anything; one day she wanted to keep her horses, the next she wished them to be sold.

Though Sidney's picture of Miss Skeffington did not altogether tally with my impressions of her, I couldn't fault his arguments for keeping the horses until they had shown their mettle. Thoroughbreds like Miss Skeffington's could command prices that would make it possible for her to 'sail to America' or anywhere else she pleased for the rest of her life, even if she lived to her father's ripe age.

I meant to keep an eye on the horses' training, on their performance on race-courses later, and on Sidney. There was always a hope that Julia would phone him again. And if she did, Sidney promised, he would let me know at once.

The spring plucked sharply at my nerve-ends. The sight of Oberon enjoying Sheba depressed me; the spectacle of Tiger aglow with the importance of *Three Brassieres to Bond Street* instead of Claire's wistful charms infuriated me; the swiftness of the Duke's hound and the Hoopers' ponies made me feel I was plodding along to no purpose.

The plodding got heavier every day. With daffodils unfurling, horse-chestnuts putting up their candles, and city-workers making love in the parks, the animal-owners came pouring into the surgery asking me to 'doctor' their bitches and pussies.

Miss Shaw brought her semi-siamese Tom because someone had told her 'doctoring' would cure his passion for fighting. Despite his cauliflower-ear Tom had grown into a handsome lilac-pointed animal. Muriel was pleased with his influence on Miss Shaw.

'You know, Michael,' she said, 'they say you can't teach an old dog new tricks. I always thought it should go on 'nor can you persuade an old owner to accept a new pet.' But Miss Shaw's an exception. She really has got over losing Andy.'

Spring made the Armstrongs' fox throw caution to the winds. He had broken his truce with the white cat and I had to go and stitch up his cheek. That was a happy visit. Peter told me Elizabeth's 'complex' had disappeared; she no longer talked of cats in her sleep. Elizabeth told me Peter's 'thing' about 'splendid wild creatures' was almost cured. After ten years of marriage and ferocious pets Peter was thinking of giving Renard to the zoo because they were expecting a baby.

Mrs Topper rang up, her little voice almost civil, and asked whether I could recommend a mate for Pooky. Immersions in cold water were, of course, effective but she had begun to wonder whether the little darling was not entitled to something – nicer. But just in case the excitement might be too much for Pooky, would I first visit him?

When I called Mr Topper was out and Mrs Topper said he rarely spent an evening at home; her husband had somehow changed in the past month or so. She was worried.

Would I go and see him at his office?

'I'm a vet,' I told her, 'not a doctor.'

'That's why I thought you'd be able to tell me what's the matter with him – I'm sure Archibald isn't ill – His trouble may have something to do with – well Pooky's problem.' The poodle was sitting in a corner, staring soulfully at a bitch in the garden opposite. 'I mean –' there was none of the usual sharpness in Mrs Topper's small voice. 'As a vet you understand sex, don't you? I have nothing to go on, but Archibald –'

Clearly Mrs Topper had given thought to making a sacrifice, the 'supreme' one of marriage. But if *I* could save her the 'trouble', she hinted, she would show her gratitude, no doubt from the depths of her big Woolworth bag.

I quickly killed that idea. There was no sign of the cat-pictures Archibald had bought or the carved dresser he had acquired at Tiger's shop. If Mr Topper had taken rooms somewhere and was celebrating a spring of his own it was none of my business. I promised Pooky a miniature poodle bitch after his own heart.

Even in Uncle Simon's Mews spring kept plucking at my nerve-ends. When Muriel took our cavalcade of dogs walking she wore a pale blue suit matching her 'new' hair and high-heeled shoes that shortened her stride; the Donizettis put tubs of wall-flowers outside the door of their house and the still vacant Number Seven; at night boys and girls who had been turfed out of the park sought the dark corners below my windows, and in the morning Joanna hung the bird-cage on a hook outside her bedroom and the song of her thrush made the people in my surgery lift their heads and talk of summer.

Both Muriel and I were so used to Joanna's presence in our house, Joanna dressing up the alsatian, Joanna teaching Rocco or Teddy or Pug to walk on his hindlegs, Joanna brushing one or other of them, that we failed to notice her on the day she skipped school.

I had finished my morning-surgery when Muriel said she thought she heard someone in the waiting-room; and there they were, a small boy with something wrapped up in his school-blazer and Joanna.

'Jo, why aren't you at school?' asked Muriel. 'Is it a holiday?'

'No Auntie Whiting.' Joanna plucked the boy's shirt-sleeve. 'It's Ray, you see . . . his puppy. Come on Admiral!' She unbunched Ray's blazer and brought out the smallest Chihuahua I'd ever seen, a minute pointed face, golden brown, comparatively large pointed ears, a body so fragile that Joanna held it up like a piece of Meissen china. 'It's a butterfly dog,' she said, 'that's why we called it Admiral. Ray found it in a book – the picture of the admiral butterfly.'

'Yes dear,' said Muriel, 'but who gave you permission to stay at home today?'

'S'like this,' Ray came to the defence. 'Jo said you have to do something to a puppy or it gets sick –'

Joanna nodded. 'Puppies get temper, don't they Uncle Michael?'

'Distemper; well yes.'

'So Jo said,' Ray rushed on, 'we must take Admiral to the vet and her Uncle Michael was a vet and she'd come too 'case Admiral was afraid –'

Joanna clearly had 'come too' because Ray had been afraid. Muriel shrugged her shoulders; though the children had skipped school she was on their side.

'All right,' I said, taking Admiral. 'Come in.'

'That's the surgery,' Joanna explained to Ray. 'Like doctors have.'

Admiral, I found, was not a puppy but a full-grown young bitch. 'Where did you get her?' I asked Ray.

'Mr Lightbody – the petshop; Mr Lightbody *gave* me

109

Admiral,' he added, a little defiantly. It was a funny kind of dog for a ten year old boy, and it was odd for the owner of a petshop to give away a well bred bitch.

I expected to find something wrong with her, and I did. On the right side of her throat, under the skin, I felt a hard lump and when I touched it Admiral flinched.

Joanna seemed to know about it. 'Is it mumps?' she asked.

'No, a kind of pimple. I'll take it away.'

Muriel put up the operating screen. 'Cancer?' she asked.

'I don't think so. Better be on the safe side though.'

I injected Admiral with the local anaesthetic Muriel had prepared, and the little bitch hardly stirred while Muriel held her steady. The knob of tough tissue came away easily. There seemed to be no spread of the growth but I decided to send it to the Pathology Laboratories to make sure it was not malignant. The incision I had made was so small that two stitches were sufficient to close it, and when I combed back the hair over the neck nothing showed. As I picked Admiral up she gave a sigh, curled up in my hand and went to sleep.

On the other side of the screen the children were sitting side by side on the bench I used for the examination of large dogs, Joanna – olive-skinned with black curls and dark serious eyes, Ray, a colourless little sparrow of a boy with humour about his eyes and the wide mouth of a fledgling. Involuntarily his hand had slipped into Joanna's.

'Admiral's fine,' I told them. 'Just a bit sleepy.'

'Like after the dentist?' asked Ray.

'That's right.' I gave him his animal and showed him where I'd operated. 'I've taken the – pimple away, so you must watch Admiral doesn't scratch there.'

'Ooh, I had sewings when I cut my hand.' Joanna held out her palm. 'See Ray? Then the doctor came and cut them off.'

'Yes, Admiral has two stitches in her neck. If you bring her in next Friday I'll take them out.'

Ray looked at Joanna. 'Can't,' he said, with a worried frown.

'Why not?'

'He lives in Battersea,' explained Joanna. 'He's got to go home in the school bus.'

I suddenly realised why the children had skipped school. Ray was too young to run about London on his own; the only way he could have gone to Knightsbridge with Joanna, without his parents knowing, was by pretending he had travelled in the school bus as usual.

'Ask your mother to bring you,' I suggested.

'Can't,' said Ray.

'Why not?'

'Mum's at work.'

'You can come in the evening, about six.'

'Can't, Mum's at work.'

'And your Dad?'

'Dad's not home yet.'

'When does he come home?'

'Eight.'

'Are you at home on your own until then?'

'No.'

'Where do you go?'

'Mr Lightbody's.'

'The petshop?'

'S'right.'

'Well, what shall we do about Admiral?' I asked. 'Shall I come to your house?'

Ray shook his head. Of course, he didn't want his parents to know he had taken Admiral to the vet instead of going to school. 'All right, I'll see Admiral at Mr Lightbody's,' I promised.

'Auntie Whiting,' Joanna was looking at her watch,

'please can we stay with you?'

Muriel turned away to hide her smile. 'So you can pretend you've been to school?'

'Yes please.'

'Just this once then – if you promise not to do it again. And Ray – you're not to run away. I'm going to take you to the bus after tea, and no nonsense.'

'It's nothing serious, sir, is it?' asked Mr Lightbody, his big bloodhound-face dropping another inch.

'No; I had it analysed, it wasn't a cancer.'

'Well, that's a relief.' He put a handful of lettuce-leaves inside a cage of guineapigs, and carefully refastened the doors. 'People are funny about animals. *I* should know – thirty years in the Army Vet Corps; and I've seen a whole regiment down in the dumps because the regimental goat died of old age. You wouldn't credit it sir, would you? – and that boy!' Mr Lightbody's pendulous cheeks wobbled. 'Break his heart it would if anything happened to the little bitch. I'd have given him the terrier over there or the spaniel pup if he'd wanted them; but no, nothing would do but the butterfly bitch.'

'Where did she come from?'

'She belonged to an old lady on the other side of the river – a real posh old lady she was; used to buy dog-biscuits in my shop. Well, she died and her daughter didn't want the bitch – said she was out all day and it wasn't fair keeping an animal shut in a flat. Now Ray – he takes Admiral out walking every morning before he goes to school – plays with her when he gets back until his father comes home. A fine state he was in today when his Dad said he was coming home at six, and *you* expected *after* six. But we sorted it out between us.' The old man grinned. 'I said I'd give him an alibi as you might call it. He's going to tell his Dad you cut out that lump in my shop – you don't mind sir, do you?' He gave

112

me no time for an answer. 'It's not that I hold with that sort of thing, sir, but the boy couldn't help himself. His Mum or his Dad wouldn't take the bitch to a vet; Ray knew that. Nor would they phone for a vet to go to their house. But it'll be all right your going there *now* – like you come over from my shop, see? You might have treated one of *my* dogs, not that Mr Ellis will ask any questions. Worn out he is when he gets home.'

'By what Ray told me both his parents seem to be working pretty hard.'

'Overtime,' said Mr Lightbody. 'Both of them are doing plenty of overtime – Mr Ellis works on electrical parts and his Missus in a canteen. Don't see much of each other, they don't. Mr Ellis comes home at eight and the Missus goes to work at teatime. So Ray can't get in until his Dad's home.'

'What does he do with himself?'

'Winter he's in here, come summer he plays in the street. Buys himself lollies and packets of chips when he's hungry. He's not short of cash that boy.'

'Seems to me he's short of parents.'

'Well sir, it's the way things are nowadays – though I *will* say bringing up a boy like the Ellis's do wouldn't have done when *I* was a kid. The neighbours would have talked – in a nice street that is. But nowadays they're all doing the same thing – money – money, that's all they think of. And what for! You'll see for yourself sir. There's nothing the Ellis's haven't got – a TV set with a twenty-one inch screen, a washing-machine, spin-dryer, a cine-projector, deep-freeze, transistor wireless sets. Well, they got to do overtime to keep up the payments.'

'You mean everything's bought on tick?'

'On the never-never, the whole lot. Well, maybe they pay cash for the books they have lying about the parlour.'

'Books? Do they have time for reading?' I wondered when.

113

'Oh, I don't know as they *read* sir, but they've got books; every one of them by a titled lady or gentleman – *you* know sir, Lord Russell and Princess Marie Louise, Sir Winston Churchill, Sir Anthony Eden, Lady Diana Cooper –' Mr Lightbody suddenly became thoughtful. 'Well, now the one thing *I'd* like to read's that Lady Chatterley. Maybe I'm wrong, maybe you *can* get books on the never-never, because *everyone's* got them books by the titled ladies and gentlemen – the lot of them, up and down the road.'

The road, cheap sulphur-yellow brick, cowered between the beautiful Battersea power-station and the fine new flats on the North Bank of the river. Against the dark sky the new flats, their windows ablaze with lights, looked like a mighty colonnade of soaring flaring pillars of fire on a fabulous stage. Their glittering reflections in the river drowned the sober lamps of barges and warehouses, the dusty dim street-lights along the dingy brick houses on the South Bank.

But Ray's road looked prosperous, with television aerials moaning from the rooftops, spring flowers bobbing from window-boxes, front doors whose fresh paint shone in the Silver Ghost's headlamps. Ray's house had a glass door with an ornamental iron grill; the bell gave one of those synthetic-ally sweet expensive chimes.

Ray himself answered it. 'Did Mr Lightbody tell you?' he asked.

'Don't worry, I've got our story pat.'

'O.K.,' said Ray in a tough Wagon Train voice, 'come right in Mister.'

Mr Ellis and Admiral were sitting in front of the TV set. Mr Ellis was asleep, Admiral opened her eyes when the fast gunman on the screen began depleting the rows of bottles behind the bar. Admiral didn't like that; she jumped off the settee and crept underneath.

Ray went and got her out, a minute bundle of golden-brown fur with a pair of large shuddering ears. He cuddled and stroked her, and whispered in some private language until the ears had calmed down. The incision on Admiral's neck had healed and I was able to remove the stitches. When I touched the spot where the lump had been and the area around it, the little animal gave no sign of tenderness or pain.

I was about to go when the fast gunman set about overturning the bar tables, one by one, with the dreariness of a pedantic. The repeated crashes wakened Mr Ellis. He sat up, rubbing his bloodshot eyes, saw me, and got up.

'That's Mr Morton, Dad,' said Ray.

'I'm sorry, sir.' He shook hands with me. 'Why didn't you call me, silly boy. My nipper been a nuisance, sir?'

'Not a bit – he was quite right. Admiral will be sounder without that lump.'

'Ray, have you paid the doctor?'

'S'on the National Health,' said Ray.

'Don't be daft, boy. The National Health is for *people*. Get out your money. Come on – you don't think *I'm* going to pay for your dog, do you?'

'How much?' asked Ray, manfully.

I remembered that Ray was supposed to be well supplied with pocket-money. 'Twenty pence?' I had to charge *something*; the boy's father seemed set on making him pay up.

Without a word Ray delved into his pockets, brought out a couple of coins, and handed them over.

He did not speak until we were out of the living-room and he'd opened the front door. There he hovered, clearly not yet willing to let me go.

'Well Ray, what is it?' I asked him.

'I was going to the circus tomorrow,' he said, flatly.

'A circus? Where?'

Ray produced a crumpled handbill. It advertised Vittorio Strada's 'world-famous' circus presenting 'the greatest variety of wild animals ever seen', and 'the finest artistes of

115

Europe, Africa, America and India'. India . . . snakes . . .
snake-dancers; I'd almost forgotten the Duke's brainwave
. . . Julia in a circus? Well, I was going to take a look at
Vittorio Strada's anyway. It had pitched tents beside some
Battersea playing fields.

'Where is it?'

Ray pointed across the rooftops. There was a pink glow
in the sky, possibly a reflection of the circus lights. 'I was
going tomorrow,' he repeated, rather sadly.

'Have you spent all your money?'

He nodded.

'Here you are then.' I gave him back his coins not caring
whether I ruined Mr Ellis's pedagogic efforts or not.

'Gee, thanks Mister,' said Ray, in his best Wagon Train
voice. '*You're* great!'

Vittorio Strada's 'world-famous' circus stood on a patch
of mud between the railed-off football pitch and tenements
which were in process of being dismantled by a firm called
Courage Demolitions. The voice of a lion, somewhat depressed and disgruntled, echoed weirdly behind heaps of rubble
and skeins of rusty water-pipes.

I followed a bunch of teenagers across the slippery planks
to the big tent, which looked about the size of a modest tea-
stall at a country fair. Surprisingly the tent did hold between
two and three hundred people around the small ring. I
managed to squeeze in at the end of the first row, where boys
and girls in jeans had begun a slow handclap. The clapping
almost upset our wooden bench, digging it more deeply into
the mud until it came to rest on the cinders beneath.

'Careful now!' exclaimed a man behind us.

'There are people sitting behind you,' said an irate Mum
with two little girls. 'Them as don't know 'ow to behave in
public 'ave no business to come 'ere.'

My teenage neighbours giggled and went on clapping until

116

a rider in the centre of the ring blew his hunting horn and the five-man band at the far end struck up the time-honoured pom pom tiddle-tiddle pom pom pom pom, pom pom tiddle-tiddle . . . My neighbours at last sat still and gave me a chance of studying the programme.

I couldn't imagine where Vittorio Strada had managed to tick away his camels and elephants, lions and horses, but according to the programme they and many other animals were to perform 'miracles of artifice, supported by tightrope artistes Pietro and Bella, the celebrated clown Cosimo and his many sons, the astonishment of India – Dara Devi with her dangerous snake –'

The beating of my heart almost choked me. Dara Devi, Lakshmi – it *had* to be Julia; and if it was, India had every right to be 'astonished'. So overwhelming was the thought of Julia that I submitted to the biting of a persistent flea without making any attempt at killing it.

CHAPTER EIGHT

The flea kept biting me, the clowns kept tumbling, seals balanced balls on their noses, lions made a show of ferocity, and then Dara Devi and her 'dangersome' snake took the ring and I forgot about the flea.

Dara Devi-Julia, to the accompaniment of bagpipe squeals, stretched her brown arms in a slow snake-like motion. Her little body, dressed in imitation pantherskin tights and bolero, wiggled the usual invitation to Cobby at her feet and the snake began to climb up her right leg, round her waist and across the outstretched arms. The audience was watching with bated breath; even the beatniks beside me had stopped chewing gum.

The first of her dances accomplished Julia bowed and a roll of drums invited the audience to applaud. It did, loudly enough for my purposes. I started to whistle 'On Ilkley Moor baht 'at' and Cobby, who had finished her first act hanging limply round Julia's neck, lifted her head and began to slide to the ground.

Julia grabbed the remaining third of the snake and spoke to her, glancing in my direction. She looked as worried as I meant her to be. The lights went out again, leaving only a bright pool for Julia in the centre of the ring. I went on whistling despite the vociferous annoyance of the Mum behind me who kept muttering something about 'people as don't know 'ow to behave in public'.

Cobby, irresistibly drawn to 'Ilkley Moor', had succeeded in disengaging herself from Julia's hands and had reached a point outside the illuminated circle. Julia, unwilling to draw her public's attention to this unrehearsed incident, went on dancing on her own but she kept moving closer and closer to the edge of the ring in Cobby's direction and mine. The spotlight was late in following her.

Suddenly a shrill screaming broke out along my row and the bench capsized, throwing at least a dozen of us to the ground. It was something I'd certainly not foreseen and I was extremely worried in case Cobby got hurt. I whistled 'Ilkley Moor' as loudly as I could, but the tune was drowned by the screams and shouts of the beatniks.

Julia came flying up to me. 'You . . . you rat! Listen everyone! Listen!' she shouted. 'The snake's harmless – you'll be all right! Keep quiet please! Quiet. I'll find her! Cobby! Cobby!'

The circus management had at last tumbled to it that something had gone wrong; the lion-tamer and the clowns came tearing into the ring and the band struck up the triumphal march from Carmen. Now it was quite certain that Cobby would not hear my whistling. I had to go after her, on my hands and knees.

'What's happening?'

'What's gone wrong,' people kept asking.

Some, who had found out, climbed on their benches, the benches toppled over, people toppled over, and in the middle of the pandemonium an unctuous man's voice advised the audience to 'keep yer 'eads. I've dialled nine-nine-nine and the police will be 'ere in due course.'

It was more than I'd bargained for.

I went down on my stomach and crawled through between benches and legs and bodies, whistling 'Ilkley Moor.' By now Cobby might have got anywhere in the tent.

'Take it easy!' came a reassuring voice. 'Take it easy, everybody. Don't panic!' Miraculously two policemen had arrived and were helping people to their feet.

'Take it easy,' said the indignant Mum. 'I like *that*! You

better catch that snake, Constable!'

'We're doing our best, lady – the snake's harmless, but if you're worried you'd better leave by the exit over there.'

'Leave!' The Mum clutched the hands of her girls. 'We're staying, see! I've paid for the best seats!'

'Well, you'll come to no harm, lady,' said the Constable.

'I think it's a disgrace, the Law not protecting us. And that – that circus! They've no right to 'ave an 'orrible hanimal like that if they don't know 'ow to manage it . . . And the Law . . .'

I got back down into the mud, still whistling. Suddenly I felt something slide over my legs. I called out, and Cobby came nozzling up, affectionately encircling my waist.

'Cobby!' I heard Julia's voice.

'Here Julia! I've got her.'

'Oh, Michael!' She came crawling up to us along the ground, and I grabbed her.

I was entangled with Cobby, and Cobby was likely to spit in my face with jealousy, but I took Julia in my arms and kissed her. She kissed me back, her shoulders shaking with laughter.

'Michael, you're crazy!'

'I love you.'

'I love you too – damn you.'

'Over there' shouted a man, somewhere above our heads. 'Officer, I'm sure I saw the snake over there a minute ago.'

'Over there! Over there!' shouted voices from different parts of the tent. I looked out from behind our upturned bench. The audience had occupied the well-lit ring, while police, animal-trainers and clowns were hunting among the debris and the remaining rows of benches.

'Julia, let's get out of here quick.'

'How?'

'You go first – they'll think you're still looking for Cobby.

Turn left as you go out. My car's in the first street on the right. Here's the key.'

'No, I'll stay with you. They might arrest you.'

'Don't be silly. It'll be easier for me to get away alone. Go on, Julia, I won't be long.'

I didn't know how long I'd be until I spotted one of the clowns solemnly searching the mud a few feet in front of me. I called him.

'Don't tell anyone,' I said, 'but I've got the snake.'

'What!'

'Listen, please! You can tell people in a moment. But first I must get away. Miss Dara Devi wants me to get the snake out quietly so it doesn't do any damage. You can never tell what a snake will do when it's upset – will you help?'

'Well, all right. What do you want me to do?'

'Let me have your trousers – and your hat.'

'I dunno—'

'Quick, or the snake might get away again.'

'I dunno about the trousers. I can't –'

'I'll give you mine.'

The clown chuckled. 'O.K. – what a night!' He ducked under my bench, keeping well clear of Cobby. Cobby fitted quite snugly inside his vast pants.

'All set?' he asked.

'Yes. Give me five minutes – or as long as you can before letting them know.'

'What will I say?'

'Just that Miss Dara Devi managed to catch her snake, and she's taken it away.'

I climbed out, with Cobby like a ton weight about my body, and stalked off, hat pulled down over my eyes.

At the exit, where a constable was lifting the tent-flaps, I pretended that I too was searching. My last glimpse of the circus was reassuring; the audience, standing about the ring

121

like a cocktail party crowd, was drinking the tea supplied by the management.

Whatever I tried to say to Julia she burst out laughing again. Both of us were covered in mud, but I, in my clown's trousers and hat, driving the suave Silver Ghost, must have looked like the Charlie Chaplin of the silent films at his wildest.

'Darling, *where* do you live?' I pleaded with her. 'If we don't get ourselves cleaned up we *shall* get arrested. The next policeman who sees us will probably run me in for stealing the car.'

'Bullen Street,' Julia managed to get out. 'Bullen Street, Battersea – Bullen Street, Battersea,' she sang. 'I'll tell you where –'

She made me park the car a street away from her lodgings. Her room was in one of those Victorian houses which had regained something of their former neatness. There was a light in one of the ground-floor rooms, illuminating a fussily draped nylon curtain.

'Oh dear,' said Julia, 'Mrs Molesey's in. She doesn't allow visitors. But you *can't* go home like this. Darling, try not to make a noise.'

She opened the front door as silently as a burglar, listened for a moment, and then waved me on up the stairs.

'It's all right,' she sighed, closing the door of her room behind us. Cobby lazily slid down my trouser-leg and went to her basket, curling up like a cat that had been out hunting. For once she paid no attention when I kissed Julia.

'I don't like the taste of your mud, Michael. Let's take a bath – or rather, *you* can have one. I'll wash in the basin. Mrs Molesey would think there's something odd going on if she heard more water than usual going down her drain. She's not exactly generous.'

122

'My mud's as good as yours, dear. We'll share your bath.'

Julia changed into a dressing-gown and I managed to cover up, more or less, with her beach coat. The bathroom was next door to Julia's room and we managed to get in undetected. It was the best bath I'd ever had – better than my soakings after rugger or golf. Solitary baths, I told Julia, were overrated, pitifully puritanical. The Romans had discovered that much.

Back in the small bed-sitting-room Julia made coffee, and then curled up beside me on the couch. 'How's Claire and the cats?'

'Don't you know it yet? You behaved like a bitch.'

'Well, you got yourself into the gossip columns with her – and that business with the scarf –'

'Listen my pet. You got yourself into the gossip columns with Sidney Franks – not that I don't know why. Get *this* into your fat head; Claire's the nicest girl I know – yes, nicer than you – but I don't want her. I never did want her. Besides she's going to marry Tiger.'

'Tiger! The author of *Three Brassieres to Bond Street?*'

'Yes.' I had to do some quick thinking. 'But don't you drop a brick when you meet them. Their engagement's still a secret – something to do with her parents – and publicity. You understand, don't you darling?'

'Of course, Michael darling . . . I'm sorry.' She came into my arms. 'I was so jealous – well, like Cobby.' Her body, beneath the dressing-gown was marvellously soft, her long black hair moist and sweet-scented.

'Miss Hanley!' The door flew open. A fat, grey-haired woman with hamster-cheeks stood staring at us. 'I'm surprised at you! I never thought I'd see a man in *your* room – and all undressed!'

'We're not undressed,' said Julia, flushed with embarrassment.

'Well! A man in a bathrobe! I declare! And just look at

123

you! It isn't decent! I took you in out of the kindness of my heart –'

'Seven pounds a week,' objected Julia.

'Out of the kindness of my heart,' repeated Mrs Molesey, 'and that's the thanks I get. I mean to say – having a snake to live with you is bad enough, but a *man*! I never thought I'd live to see *that* going on in my house. And after all I've done for you! Now, if you'd have had the decency to take the big room –'

'I see,' said Julia, disgustedly. 'For ten pounds you'd have allowed me my snake *and* men.'

'Well, I mean to say –'

'Don't,' I told Mrs Molesey. 'My fiancée is leaving to-night.' I went to the door and edged her out. 'If there's anything owing to you we'll settle with you after we've finished packing.'

'I must say, that's a fine way –'

I shut the door, and locked it. Julia was looking upset. 'What am I to do *now*?'

'You're coming home with me, and that's where you're going to stay.'

'Thanks, but I can afford a hotel.'

'Don't be foolish, darling. I'm not a charitable institution. Hasn't the penny dropped yet? I *want* you. Muriel's got too much to do; she'll be glad of your help. And you may as well get used to a vet's house if you're going to marry a vet.'

'Am I?'

'Certainly.'

'I didn't know it; until now you forgot to mention it.'

'I didn't forget. I was broke. I still am – I won't know what my income's going to be until my uncle gets back from Africa in four months' time.'

Julia put her arms round my neck. 'Michael, you've been as stupid as I, every bit as stupid.'

'You *will* come home with me?'

'Yes. It was awful without you.'

'You won't get much of a wage – wages of sin maybe.'

'Oh, stop worrying about money! I'm not broke. *I* don't want filthy lucre – what I want is love.'

'My God, you shall have it! As much as you can stand.'

CHAPTER NINE

'Why does it wear glasses?' asked Joanna. The markings of Cobby had puzzled her since the first morning they met.

'It's made that way,' Muriel told her. 'Cobby's a spectacle snake.'

Joanna seemed quite satisfied with this explanation. 'Poor thing,' she whispered, returning to that private world where people did not exist, 'nobody takes you walking in the park.' She fondled Cobby's head. 'And mother says I'm not to speak to you . . . you know, Mother doesn't speak to Daddy . . .'

'What a silly story,' said Muriel.

'S'not silly – Mother doesn't speak to Daddy any more 'cause she's divorcing him 'cause of cruelty – Cobby! Don't go away!' The snake, hearing our dogs, was making off.

But she'd left it too late. They came tearing into the hall with Julia trying to catch Pug by the lead. Prince had cut off Cobby's retreat and stood growling at her raised head. Cobby's head and neck dilated into the formidable hood that frightened most animals. Not so Prince. He stood his ground, nose sniffing, powerful front paws set for jumping forward, ears back.

Teddy, in true spaniel-manner, flip-flopped up and down a few feet below Cobby's irritated head; Rocco had chosen a site nearer the snake's tail and sat watching it, one paw raised, ears up on the alert; and the pug had stationed himself at the very tip of the tail and was standing there square and solid, watching every move.

Julia was about to pick up Pug's lead when I suddenly thought of a way to end this daily show of antagonism.

'Leave them alone, Julia,' I told her. 'Let's see what they do when we're not here to stop them. Come in,' I opened the surgery door, 'you too, Joanna.'

'Michael, they'll *eat* Cobby.'

'They won't.' I left the door open an inch or so, enough to see the animals without their noticing us. 'I have a theory.'

'Oh, Lord!' said Julia.

Prince gazed about the hall and stopped growling. He stalked down the line of Cobby's body, thoughtfully surveyed Teddy and Rocco, and then confronted Pug, giving a curious high-pitched bark. Pug made one or two uncertain steps towards the snake's tail-end, and visibly bracing himself grabbed it in his mouth.

Cobby turned with fantastic speed, but instead of attacking the dogs with the heavy front-part of her body she disengaged her tail, smacked Pug lightly across the nose, accurately caught Rocco and Teddy across their haunches, and tripped Prince so that he fell of a heap across her body. There was no sign of her earlier annoyance; her head, no longer hooded, had gone back to its normal size.

Pug, recovering from his surprise, shook himself and went to pick up Rocco's lead; Rocco obediently took Teddy's and Teddy picked up Prince's lead. Prince backed away from the half open door of the breakfast-room while Cobby, with leisurely dignity, made her exit.

Julia sighed with relief. 'And I thought the dogs hated Cobby.'

'I told you they didn't. It was just a slight misunderstanding. The dogs couldn't make out why Cobby wasn't going with them on their walks – a nice long thing like a super dog-lead. It didn't make sense; they felt a bit like Joanna, "poor thing, nobody takes you walking in the park". That was all.'

'Well, I don't know much about animals yet, do I, Michael? . . . except snakes.'

'Aunt Julia, can we go now?' asked Joanna. 'Pug's *waiting*.'

I watched them from the surgery window; the familiar cavalcade of Julia, with Joanna hopping beside her, holding Pug's lead, Pug holding Rocco's lead, Rocco holding Teddy's and Prince setting the pace. They were crossing the Mews, coats and hair shining in the summer sun. I thought it was the one sight that would never fail to amuse and delight me.

'What an impossible household,' said Muriel. 'Julia looks so pretty.'

'So do you when you're in charge of the cavalcade.'

'Rubbish! You don't have to keep grooming my ego; it's doing nicely on high-heels and hairdo's. Better get down to work.' The first patient was coming up the steps, a corpulent dachshund in the arms of an old lady. 'Michael, the Duke sounded worried. Try and see him before lunch.'

The Duke was more angry than worried. Grey Rainbow, looking like the champion of all greyhounds, was reclining at his master's feet, utterly indifferent to his failures.

'I'll complain to the Greyhound Racing Association!' The Duke's false teeth clacked shut, making him look as grim as he felt. 'And if those fellows don't take it up –'

'Not yet, sir,' I tried to pacify him. 'There must be a reason why both Brighton and Wolverhampton wouldn't let Rainbow run.'

'Have you found one, Morton?'

'No.' I remembered Rainbow's curious fit after his bath in the Duke's cottage. 'Not yet. But I haven't yet seen him go after a hare.'

'You shall. I want you to come down to Hazelbridge for the week-end.'

'I'd like to, if I can get away.'

'You must. Don't you see how important it is! Besides

128

there isn't only Rainbow; my sister wants you to check her horses, especially Rustler. She *has* entered him for the Horse of the Year Show. Queer thing, Molly's suddenly mad keen on jumping – can't make it out. Thought she'd grown out of the horsey stage – that's settled then.'

'I'll let you know on Friday, sir.'

'Well, don't let us down. Just had a word with Claire; she wants you to stay at her parents' place – more comfortable than my sister's. Bring your friend if you like.'

Julia was enchanted with the Claremonts' Adam house on the outskirts of Hazelbridge village, but disenchanted with our first meal of frozen chops and Coca-Cola. With Claire's parents abroad in Sweden the staff were on holiday and there was only a daily woman who seemed to do nothing but push around a noisy vacuum-cleaner. The washing-up was left to the guests, or rather to Julia.

'No, I don't want help, Michael,' she told me, smiling at Claire. My impression was that the two girls had arranged things so that Claire and I could have a 'quiet talk'. Claire had been unusually subdued for some time.

'Tiger's going to New York at the end of September,' said Claire, 'with *Three Brassieres to Bond Street*. I am to stay and look after the shop.'

'Couldn't his second-in-command do that?'

'I'd like to see the play on Broadway,' Claire hesitated, 'but Tiger hasn't asked me. He – he doesn't seem to care if we don't – about not being with me. Michael – he's twenty-two – the same age as I. Do you think he isn't – well, ready for women, or is it just me?'

'To me, at any rate, it's been clear he's in love with you ever since I've known you,' I told her.

'*I* sometimes think he is,' Claire absentmindedly stroked Chou-en-Lai's ears. 'He's kissed me – and once he stayed the night at my flat. Nothing happened.'

'That's not surprising; Tiger *would* behave like an Edwardian gentleman with the girl he's going to marry.'

"But Michael, has he ever *thought* of marrying me? You know, I did believe nothing would have to be said between us. But it isn't so simple; there's our families – my parents have money, but it's my father who made it. Grandfather was a nobody, a small shopkeeper. Tiger's people have no money, but their name's in the Doomsday Book – they're a terribly distinguished family.'

'Do you know Tiger's parents?'

'Of course. Tiger and I have been friends ever since we were children. His parents always invited me to his parties.'

'Then where's the difficulty. Don't they like you?'

'They do; I'm sure they do. But that doesn't mean they'd be pleased if Tiger wanted to marry me. I'm not as – as well bred –'

'You're being quite absurd, Claire. If there's anything at all that's characteristic about truly well bred people it is that they aren't snobs, least of all social snobs. Snobbery's the *hall-mark* of the bourgeois, the middle-class second-rates who're straining after becoming top-people. You know that's true, don't you?'

'Yes.' Claire smiled. 'Mummy's a fearful snob – but why doesn't Tiger –'

'Tiger will miss you when he's in the States. That should make him realise how he feels about you. He's a bit slow –'

'He is a poet, of course.' Claire was looking happier. 'But he does believe in a good sex life – you're right, he *is* slow in some things. I mean, he begins everything with a theory about it.'

'Well, stop theorising with him about sex life,' I told her. 'Shut him up if he starts discussing the subject intellectually.'

'Make him think I'm not *with* him?'

'Yes, that'll worry him since you usually are aiding and abetting his ideas – all the way, even down to chops and

Coca-Cola.'

'Michael, you *have* made me see things straight. You see, I went to my doctor because I couldn't sleep. But he told me there's nothing wrong with me. Julia said if there's nothing wrong with me it's a vet I should see.'

'Well, I must say that was handsome of Julia.'

In the afternoon we all watched Grey Rainbow race on the improvised track round Claire's paddock. The hare Masters had promised, had not yet materialised, but he was sure of producing it by Sunday morning. Meanwhile, Rainbow was running after one of Lady Jane's stableboys on a motorbike; according to my stop-watch his speed was phenomenal, good enough to beat Long Arrow, the current star of the tracks.

I felt as puzzled as the Duke. Rainbow was first rate. Even after hard work he showed no sign of exhaustion; his heartbeat and pulse were regular and steady, respiration slow. The dog had a stamina worthy of the best tracks in the country. I could see no reason whatever for his being turned down.

'Crooks,' said the Duke, 'that's what we're up against. Went to see them myself. Something funny going on or they'd have told me one good reason why they wouldn't let Rainbow run.'

'It's unfair,' Julia condoled with him. 'Didn't *any* of the managers tell you why?'

'No, not one. Just a polite request to take my dog home.'

'I'm sure Michael will find out why,' said Julia.

I was not at all sure, and I was grateful when Julia created a diversion by making the Duke help her unpack our picnic. Her tea and sympathy so far restored his temper that he stayed to watch Molly's performance on Rustler.

The pony had improved tremendously since I'd seen him jump during the winter. He went up to the fences in a relaxed canter and picked up his hooves with instinctive ease. Molly's timing in lifting him over and the pony's reactions worked in perfect accord.

'If Molly goes on working with him as she has done,' said Lady Jane, delightedly, 'she'll win Rustler's class at the Show; don't you think so, Mr Morton?'

'She'll stand a good chance, certainly.'

'Thought Molly'd have more sense,' muttered the Duke.

Molly on Rustler came and stood beside me when Lady Jane herself put Fairline, the second-best pony, through his paces.

'Rustler's doing all right,' she said, 'isn't he?' She stuffed a strand of hair under her hat. 'Mummy's absolutely in orbit.'

'So you've decided you like jumping, after all.'

'I don't!' Molly wrinkled her nose. 'Horses are a bore.'

I didn't know what to make of it. 'Well, nice of you to please your Mother.'

'Please Mummy!' Molly grinned. 'Oh, I'll please her, at a price. A week before the Show I'm going to tell her I won't ride, unless she lets me go to university – you won't tell her, will you?'

'No. But do you think it'll work? Your mother won't like being blackmailed.'

'She won't,' said Molly. 'She'll agree though, I know she will. She wouldn't find another rider – not anyone who can handle Rusty as well as I can – inside a week.'

Lady Jane turned out early on the following morning to see the final trials of her brother's greyhound, sure that he would not do as well as on the previous day; the Duke arrived full of confidence, discussing the letter of complaint he'd sent to the Greyhound Racing Association.

It seemed incongruous to feel tension on such a morning, with the quiet paddock veiled in dew, the Downs sleepily

132

casting off the heat-haze, and larks rising from a kaleido-scope of fields.

But the Duke's excitement was infectious. I could hardly hold Grey Rainbow; the dog was straining like a thing possessed, while Masters ran the motorbike round the path, and then checked his improvisations. At a certain speed, Masters was to pull a wire on his handlebars which in turn would release the hare on a thirty foot rope. I had seen it work the night before, and the contraption did seem the nearest thing to an electric hare on a proper dogtrack.

Masters passed our 'grandstand' and raised his arm.

'Let go,' shouted the Duke.

Rainbow leaped after the motorbike, like a spring un-coiling, back arched, legs flying out, neck stretched horizon-tally. For fifty yards he sprinted like a champion, with the Duke cheering him on and even Lady Jane putting the binoculars to her eyes. Then, suddenly Rainbow turned a somersault; I could see through my glasses that he'd reached the hare, tried to pull up, and that his own impetus had thrown him, because the natural brakes couldn't have func-tioned at such speed.

But the dog was unhurt. He picked himself up and raced off . . . in the opposite direction from the hare. He came dashing up to the Duke, lay down at his feet, and began to shiver and whimper. It was a fit of 'nerves', exactly like the one I'd witnessed months ago at the cottage.

Without a word, the Duke and Lady Jane watched me examine Rainbow. 'He's not hurt,' I told them.

'What was it?' asked the Duke, miserably. 'What can have got into him?'

'He didn't like the hare.'

Masters came driving up, the hare already back in the saddlebag. I took it out and threw it to Rainbow. The dog backed away and almost wept, crawling on his belly behind Lady Jane's pony.

133

'Take it away, Masters,' said the Duke. 'Very well, so he doesn't like *this* hare. What does it prove? Nothing.'

I now felt certain of what I'd known subconsciously, since Masters had told me Rainbow would never race on a track. I thought it would be unfair to withhold my knowledge from Rainbow's owner. 'Let's go back to the cottage,' I suggested. 'I think I can show you what's the matter with the dog.'

'Yes,' said Lady Jane. 'I think you should know, Dick.'

Rainbow followed us, apparently completely recovered from the fall and the shakes. In the living-room at the cottage, I again checked his heartbeat and pulse; they were steady and normal.

'Masters, would you please give me the gloves his Grace wears for cooking?' I asked.

'Do as Mr Morton says,' the Duke told his hesitant major-domo. 'They're in the dresser, aren't they?'

Masters rummaged for a while and then produced a pair of cotton gardening gloves.

'No, not these,' I said. 'You wore gauntlets, sir.'

'Of course I did.' The Duke went to the dresser, edging Masters out of the way. 'These are the ones,' he said, handing me the greasy pair. 'You're losing your memory, Masters.'

'Now, will you watch, sir?' I said. 'Rainbow! Here boy!' The dog got up. 'Catch!' I threw him the gloves. Rainbow gave one sniff, howled, and crawled into the farthest corner of the room. He was again shivering uncontrollably.

'I don't understand. What is it, Morton?' The Duke squatted beside the dog, fondling him, touching his nose.

'Rainbow's allergic to hares . . . even to rabbits,' I said. 'Your gloves are lined with rabbit fur; he reacted to them the first time I saw him here, do you remember? I'm afraid there's no doubt, is there Masters?'

'No, sir,' Masters admitted.

The Duke looked up. 'You *knew*, Masters! Why didn't

134

you tell me?'

'I didn't want to upset your Grace.'

'That was wrong of you, Masters – I suppose the managers of the race-tracks didn't want to upset me either.'

'So it seems,' I said. It was futile to leave any doubt in the Duke's mind. He was still calming his shivering hound, with pity and gentleness.

'Best thing,' said Lady Jane, 'is to sell Rainbow. Take my advice Dick. The dog's already cost you more than you can afford. I dare say Rainbow'll be all right for breeding; you might get a good price.'

'Sell Rainbow!' The Duke rose to his full height. 'Get rid of a fine dog just because he's a – an invalid! Certainly not!'

'Hardly an invalid,' said Lady Jane. 'He's useless for doing the job he's meant to do. You got him for racing – to *pay*. It's a pity, but he won't pay. Dick, why not forget about greyhounds; horses are much more rewarding.'

'Horses!' The Duke's voice was full of contempt. 'Jane, as you very well know, horses have been the downfall of the Alanspring family.'

'Horses,' said the Duke a few days later when I went to see him at his town flat, 'horses *may* serve a purpose. It remains to be seen.'

It was all very mysterious. I had fully expected to find the old man in despair. He'd taken the revelation of Rainbow's allergy with fortitude, so much so that I had been afraid he'd suffer a reaction. Instead, he seemed almost hopeful, and his attitude towards Rainbow was more paternal than ever. Rainbow, I noticed, had been given a cushier quilt for his bed.

'I've done some reading about dogs,' the Duke told me. 'An allergy, in a case like Rainbow's, would be a mental – er – aberration, wouldn't it?'

'Possibly. But I'm not going to tell you Rainbow's allergy

is due to his mother having been scared by a buck rabbit.'

'Then you don't believe in psychiatry?'

'Not for animals. The communication between animals and people is too imperfect – among other difficulties.'

'But in America there are animal-psychiatrists.'

'*Any* vet should be able to cure a *simple* hysteria if the cause of it can be removed.'

'Precisely.' The Duke leaned forward in his chair, all triumph and eagerness. 'I must find someone who can remove Rainbow's – well, the root of his fear.'

'The root of his *allergy* is hare or rabbit. If there's none around, Rainbow's a lovely runner – not a bit hysterical. Hysteria and allergy are not synonymous.'

'But they *might* be?'

'Occasionally – in humans.'

'Well then, I know what I must do – thought of it right away. I'll take Rainbow to America – to a good psychiatrist. Don't misunderstand me, Morton. You'll still be in charge when we return. After all it's you who made the diagnosis. Thing is, that dog of mine's meant to race, and I'll see he does. I'll take him to the States as soon as I can afford it – as I was saying, horses may serve their purpose. Went to a meeting with my sister – won fifty pounds – outsider at Kempton Park.'

CHAPTER TEN

The race that won the Duke fifty pounds should have been a walk-over for Miss Skeffington's Cybele. But Cybele hadn't even been placed; she was last but one. The recent history of the Skeffington horses was beginning to bother me. Septimus had been last at Ascot, and nowhere near being placed at other races. Cybele had achieved a third place at Goodwood and nothing since.

It didn't make sense. When I'd seen the horses a month or so earlier they had been fit, and as far as I could judge, well trained. Sidney told me they required still more training, but he'd have them in top form by the end of the summer. It meant Sidney should not have spent so much of his time in London or at races in which neither of the Skeffington horses were running.

But it was not my job to supervise Sidney Franks in an occupation he obviously understood. All I could do was have a talk with Miss Skeffington and make sure the horses' physical condition left nothing to be desired.

I rang Craftley, and told Miss Skeffington I was coming down. She sounded pleased; such a coincidence, she said, dear Sidney was going to telephone me; he was a little troubled about Cybele.

I, too, was 'troubled' when I saw Cybele walk. She was lame, her right foreleg was obviously hurting her, and on close examination, I discovered a stone wedged underneath the coronet of the hoof, which must have been there for several days. The skin over the metacarpal bones showed small fibrous thickenings, an indication that Cybele had been temporarily lame on more than one occasion.

As usual, Sidney was not present when I carried out the examination, and Jake said he could not account for Cybele's lameness.

'Haven't you been riding her?' I asked him.

'No sir, we have a wee girl exercising the filly.'

'Then tell her to clean out the hoofs before she takes Cybele out.'

'Och, I'm sure Lizzie's done that.' Jake sounded aggrieved. 'She's a fine wee rider.' Presumably, Lizzie was the girl Jake had been kissing at the window above the garage. I wondered, irrelevantly, whether *she* was a wearer of winkle-pickers, like Jake. Those pin-point shoes and horse-training somehow didn't go together.

I gave Cybele an injection of Prednisolone to deal with the inflammation, and gave Jake a prescription for more. 'Jake, was she lame after the race at Goodwood?' I asked him.

'I shouldna say so.'

'Was she, or not?'

'Aye, a wee bit,' he admitted. 'Sir, it's Septimus that's been scunnered though. He's been making a rare row in his box.'

Septimus, I found, was entirely fit except for showing more of the whites of his eyes than he used to. I had considered him an even-tempered colt, certainly without vice, but now he was looking nervous and temperamental. Jake said he was off his food. There *was* a case for a sedative, and I let Jake have another prescription.

Happiest of the animals was Sheba, now proudly pregnant, who had Oberon to herself, and was enjoying as full a sex life as any nymphomaniac could wish. Though nymphomania in a mare is usually an unsoundness, I still could find nothing wrong with that black beauty. It simply was her nature to require the frequent services of a stallion. Winsome, her daughter, seemed to have inherited Sheba's erotic

138

disposition, and Jake told me he sometimes found it difficult to keep the filly away from Septimus. Whether that was true or not, I did not think Septimus' sudden signs of nervousness had anything to do with suppressed sexual desires; his age and the rigorous training were bound to save him from Winsome's blandishments.

I walked across to the Manor House still conjecturing about Septimus' display of 'nerves'. Was he being worked too hard? Was he being given the wrong food? Short of watching him several days running, which would take more time than I could afford to spend out of London, I could only rely on sedatives and on Sidney Frank's common sense.

'Poor Sidney,' said Miss Skeffington. 'So disheartening for him after all his work. He did so hope Cybele would win at Goodwood.'

We were having sardine sandwiches and lapsang tea in her kitchen. 'Was Cybele's right foreleg giving trouble?' I asked.

'No.' Miss Skeffington frowned. 'I'm sure it was the left foreleg that was lame after the race.'

'You, yourself noticed it?'

'Oh, yes, Mr Morton. I spoke to Sidney about it because I felt certain the filly was in pain.' That sounded somewhat worse than Jake's 'a wee bit'. 'Dear Sidney's had such bad luck this season.'

'They're your horses, Miss Skeffington.'

'Yes, that's what makes it so distressing for him. He knows how anxious I am to sell my horses; and now this nice American – Mr Allerton Newtonson – is coming to England. Such an opportunity for us.'

'When are you expecting him?'

'He hopes to be here by next Saturday – he particularly wants to see our horses run at Windsor. Mr Morton, will Cybele be fit?'

'The lameness will have cleared up.'

'Splendid. Then I'll tell Sidney not to worry.'

On my way past the stables I saw Sidney's Alfa Romeo at the garage and decided to have a word with him, I climbed the outside stairway and knocked at the half-open door. Sidney, by the sound of his voice, was dressing down Jake and Jake was answering back with aggressive sullenness.

Before I could knock again a girl came running out, a thin-faced blonde as small and dainty as a whippet. 'Captain Franks!' she called out in a surprisingly penetrating voice. 'Someone at the door.' She gave me a half-smile and clattered down towards the stables.

Sidney came to the door. 'Ah, Michael! Glad you've come – Jake, off you go now. And remember what I said – come in, Michael. We're a bit primitive here, but I can offer you a drink. What will you have?'

'I'd like a beer.'

Sidney took the beer from a large refrigerator that was built into a cocktail cabinet the size of a wardrobe; not exactly primitive. Nor was the TV set with the twenty-one inch screen or the lounge-suite covered in a nylon-fur imitation of panther-skin. The whole place was expensively luxurious and somewhat effeminate.

'You don't mind beer iced, do you?' asked Sidney. 'I got used to it in America – much more sensible in hot weather; not that it's hot now. Down the hatch!'

'Miss Skeffington could do with an apartment like this,' I said.

Sidney laughed. 'She isn't the best of house-keepers, is she? But she's quite happy in her kitchen – what I want to do is enlarge this place. There's only one room for Jake and myself, and a bathroom and kitchen. We need at least one other room – especially if Jake goes on laying girls, the stupid boy. I'll enlarge the garage and build over the top; might even run to a set of pillars with a terrace.'

'You'll stay on even if Miss Skeffington sells her horses?'

Sidney glanced at me over the rim of his tankard. 'The old girl would be lost without me – there's quite a bit of land, you know, the orchards – the place would run to pot in no time if I didn't keep an eye on things. Miss Skeff's pretty helpless.'

'Especially as regards the horses.'

'Well we've been unlucky.'

'Cybele should get over her lameness in good time for the Windsor meeting.'

'Oh, Miss Skeff told you she's running – well, glad you're satisfied with Cybele.'

'I'm not,' I told Sidney. 'That type of lameness is due to carelessness.'

'Yes, I've dealt with Jake – and that girl.'

'Will Septimus be running too?'

'He's been temperamental lately. Well, you've seen him.'

'I've given Jake a prescription for a sedative.'

'All right, there's still time. If he calms down I'll have him out at Windsor.'

I was determined to see the Skeffington horses before the race, but as Julia and I were getting into the car the old lady with her dachshund arrived. While Muriel put her in the waiting-room I rang Phil Brogan. As I had expected he was attending the Roger Blandings' horses at Windsor.

I asked him to take a look at Septimus and Cybele on my behalf and to explain to Sidney, if necessary, that I'd been delayed.

'Not taking any chances?' asked Phil. 'Well, I think you're right.'

'Cybele's been lame, and Septimus tends to be a bit nervous.'

'Unlucky, aren't they? That's what *I* found.' Phil paused. 'Anyway don't worry. I'll keep an eye on them.'

141

Hans, the old dachshund, was a sad case of asthma and blindness plus an anal abscess that was causing him a good deal of pain. He was a smelly, miserable old dog, yet instead of putting him out of his misery for good, I had to keep him going. Once again it was a case of an animal being the sole companion of a lonely aged woman.

She had nursed Hans devotedly, sitting up with him at night, making hot compresses to relieve the pain, but in the end she knew I'd have to drain the abscess by making an incision. Like other clients in the same position she had left the operation to the last moment.

While Julia gave her a cup of tea in the breakfast-room Muriel and I worked on the dog. There had been no problem in opening the abscess, but it took us more than half an hour to bring him out of the anaesthetic. The poor creature had no more than a few months to live, yet I was aware how much those months could mean to an owner.

By the time we left, the Windsor meeting was due to start. We did not arrive until after the third race in which Cybele had been placed second; not bad after her lameness.

'What a pity Mr Allerton Newtonson didn't see Cybele,' said Miss Skeffington. 'She looked so pretty.'

Sidney accompanied us to the enclosure. 'Yes, she did well – Newtonson should be here in time to see Septimus; he's driving here straight from the airport.'

'Mr Morton,' Miss Skeffington had taken Julia's arm. 'I'd like you and your charming fiancée to have a little dinner with me after the races. Oh, not at my house; I'm afraid I'm not equipped for guests. We shall be dining at Three Winds – the guest-house on the London Road. You'll come Miss Hanley, won't you? I'm sure you'll enjoy meeting Mr Newtonson – such a nice American.'

'We'd love it,' said Julia. 'But we'll have to ring up London first.'

'Surely Mr Morton's clients won't expect him to work on

142

a Saturday evening – but people are so unreasonable.'

I wandered off in search of Phil Brogan. People, wearing all colours of the rainbow, were milling about in the sun, the country looked tropically green and rich, and a warm breeze carried the scents of clover and crushed grass. It was a perfect day; even bookies and tipsters were enjoying themselves.

Phil was supervising the saddling of Roger Blandings' Lordling. He looked up with a grin. 'All's well so far. Cybele wasn't doped.'

'What do you think of Septimus? He's jumpy.'

'I'd let him run.'

'I suppose so. Thanks Phil.'

'All right. If old Blandings acquires a pussy for his town-flat you can repay my kindness.'

Passing the line of bookies I bumped into Lady Jane and the Duke.

'Any tip from the horse's mouth?' he asked me.

'Sorry, today it's anyone's race.'

The Duke patted his briefcase pocket. 'I'm up twenty.'

'Beginner's luck,' said Lady Jane. 'I'm down.'

'What do you think of Septimus?' The Duke held out his race-card. 'Rather fancy that colt.'

'Not today,' I told him, with a twinge of conscience.

'Ah, well, *you* should know.'

When I returned to the enclosure Julia was talking animatedly to Allerton Newtonson whose grey wild silk suit proclaimed him as positively as if he'd been flying the Stars and Stripes. But Miss Skeffington had not, I thought, misjudged him; he was friendly and curious about people and pleased to be back in England.

'Michael,' Julia's eyes lit up in the sun. 'Mr Newtonson's been telling me about American snakes – they have about fifty species. Isn't it wonderful?'

'I guess not, ma'am,' said Mr Newtonson, 'unless you're a

143

naturalist. They're real poisonous. A tame cobra –'

His voice was drowned by the loudspeaker above our heads announcing the fifth race. Sidney joined us and gave Miss Skeffington her tote tickets for Septimus. The bulge of his right-hand breast-pocket showed he was having a successful day.

'Sidney, my dear,' said Miss Skeffington, 'may I have my binoculars?'

'They're under starter's orders! . . . They're off!'

Had I given the Duke the wrong tip? Septimus was among the first three, making for a place at the rails. Halfway round the course, where the ground rises, he was still battling with the two leaders. The jockey was standing up in the stirrups, giving the colt his head. I liked Bakewell's riding.

Suddenly, for no apparent reason, Septimus stumbled. Bakewell kept the cold's head up and he did not fall, but he seemed to lose all interest in the race. He turned side-on to the track and began dancing into the breeze like a slap-happy circus horse. He was losing ground. After his initial burst of speed it was maddening to see one horse after another pass Septimus until he was left behind, a lone straggler being jeered by disappointed backers. 'Take your time, sonny!' 'Wakey wakey!'

Anyone who didn't know Septimus must have thought he was one of those good-looking dandies without stamina. But I had seen him half an hour earlier. Only one thing could have broken his speed half way through that race, a certain kind of drug, possibly tranquiline 13B. I had not prescribed any such thing.

What was I to do? Make tests, confirm my opinion, and start a scandal which would make Miss Skeffington miserable and spoil her chances of selling the horses? A talk with Sidney? He would, of course, deny tampering with Septimus, blame 'a person or persons unknown'. I decided there was nothing I could do except keep a closer watch on the horses at future races. Besides, *could* I be a hundred per cent certain Septimus had been doped? In ninety-nine cases out of a hundred Septimus' behaviour would have been typical of an animal doped with tranquilliser, but in the hundredth case it might genuinely be accounted for by 'nervous disposition.' I began to doubt my own judgement.

'Well, that was mighty queer,' Allerton Newtonson had joined me in the paddock. He was closely watching my reaction to his remark. 'Don't you think it was?'

'Septimus wasn't yet ready for this race.'

'Well, *you* are the vet.' It didn't sound as sceptical as it might have done, especially when Newtonson gave the jockey a friendly wave. 'I'm sure sorry for Miss Skeffington – if I'd bought Septimus last year he'd be the best colt racing in the States right now.'

I too felt sorry for Miss Skeffington. 'If you *don't* buy him,' I said, 'he'll soon be the best colt racing in *England*, despite his performance today.'

'You think so?' Newtonson's question gave me no indication of his thoughts. Did he mean the colt was still worth buying, or had he already decided to let England have him? 'A Chinese lacquer screen,' said Newtonson, 'that's what I'm supposed to buy while I'm here. My wife's nuts about Chinese antiques.'

'I might be able to help you,' I told him.

'Is that so?' He sounded almost relieved. 'You know where I can get that kinda thing?'

'I have a friend with a shop in Chelsea; they specialise in Oriental antiques. I'll ask them if you like.'

'Well, that's real kind of you Mr Morton. I don't fancy window-shopping all over London.'

Julia came running out of the stables. 'Michael, I've been looking for you everywhere. It's no good, we've *got* to go home. Muriel's had two phone calls.'

'I'm sorry,' said Allerton Newtonson, 'but I hope I'll have the pleasure of your company for dinner another day. I'll be calling you . . . If you hear of a Chinese screen, I'll be staying at the Dorchester. I won't forget the snake book, Miss Hanley. I'm sending my wife a cable.'

'Snake book?' I asked Julia.

'Yes, he insisted I must have his book on American reptiles. He's one of those nice thorough people who keep promises.'

'He hasn't promised to buy Miss Skeff's horses.'

'What went wrong, Michael?'

'I don't know yet.'

'I told Muriel we're coming home right away.'

'That's all right. I'm not testing Septimus today. Who rang?'

'You'll just love this – Mrs Topper.'

'And the other call?'

'A Mr Archibald. Muriel said a new scalp for the practice.'

CHAPTER ELEVEN

'It seems you're more interested in horses than in dogs.'
Mrs Topper, oddly enough, did not sound quite as virulent
as usual. Her little voice had lost some of its sharpness.
'You're never in London nowadays, are you?'

'I'm not often *out* of London.'

'Well, I suppose you too need fresh air.' She had just
returned from a solitary holiday in Switzerland. 'Just look at
the poor darling!' She picked up her white poodle and
smothered him with kisses. 'Mummy shouldn't have left you
– what did the wicked people do to 'em?'

'Pooky's perfectly well,' I told her, 'a little thin, that's all.'

'These kennels charged the earth and then they had the
nerve to starve my dog. I have a good mind to report them
to the R.S.P.C.A.'

'They'd tell you there's no cause for complaint. The dog
ate a bit less than usual, probably because he missed his
home. Poodles often do.'

'I wish *men* did.' Mrs Topper sounded so bitter that I
almost felt sorry for her. 'My husband doesn't seem to need
a home at all nowadays – not even at night. Mr Morton,
you haven't by any chance seen his cat? He's taken it away
– somewhere.'

'No, I haven't seen either Mr Topper or his cat.'

'He said he's keeping it at his office. I know it's untrue. I
do wish you'd go and see him.'

'Mrs Topper, I told you I can't do that.'

'But I think he needs help – he – he's been so odd. When
he *is* here he looks worried. There's something on his mind,
and it's giving him no peace – I believe he's leading a double

147

life, Mr Morton. He has a mistress – some frightful alley-cat – probably someone who's making him pay hard cash for her favours.' Mrs Topper's voice became thick with hatred. 'I could strangle women of that kind! She's ruining his health – I've never seen him look so thin and drawn –'

'You may be upsetting yourself for nothing.'

'I *know* him. I'm his wife.' I was thinking she hadn't been much of a wife; it seemed to occur to her as well. 'I admit I haven't always been – as considerate as I might have been, but is that enough reason for him to destroy our marriage? We used to have lovely times together when we were younger – Italy in the summer, ski-ing in winter – in those days he wouldn't have let me go to Switzerland alone. He wouldn't have gone anywhere without me. When we had a party we used to do the cooking together – dishes we'd discovered abroad, and –'

'I'm awfully sorry, Mrs Topper, but I have another animal to see tonight. Anyway, don't worry about Pooky.'

She got up, and meekly followed me out. 'Mr Morton, I know I'm a pest – but won't you visit my husband at his office?'

'You mustn't think your husband's a case for a vet.' I tried to make it sound like a joke. It fell flat of course. 'Get him to see a doctor.'

'I can't *get* him to do anything these days – if I could lay my hands on that alley-cat of his I'd murder her.'

Mr Topper didn't have one alley-cat; he had three, none of them human. Mr Archibald, the new client for whose sake we had come dashing back from Windsor, *was* Mr Topper, but a very different Topper from the respectable Hampstead householder I had known.

He had installed himself in a couple of rooms at the top of a down-at-heel house in Gower Street, and he'd rented them because they gave out on a fire-escape 'handy for the pussies'. The pussies, apart from his own grey, were the toughest looking strays I'd seen for a long time, the tom, a brawler minus ears with big scars all over his body, the she-cat, a skinny mean-looking ginger with claws permanently at the ready.

'It was bound to happen,' said Topper, gazing at his grey Sally who was in labour with a tummyful of kittens. 'She's taken to spending the nights out like the other two but it's against her upbringing – she got out of condition, and now she's in trouble. Ginger's kittens were born inside a few minutes.'

Sally had been in labour for hours and she was exhausted. She hardly moved when I rolled her on her back and began to manipulate, but her yellow eyes were wide open, watching me with an expression of almost human resignation.

It was half an hour before I got her muscles working again and then, with the help of massage, the kittens came away. There were four of them and as soon as they were born Sally, with a gallant effort, made herself lift her head and began to lick them clean.

'Have you any brandy!' I asked Topper.

'No, only whisky.'

'That'll do.' I put a few drops in milk and gave the saucer to the mother cat. Though she didn't like the smell of it she drank, instinctively aware that she needed a 'tonic'.

Topper, looking as haggard as a new father, poured whisky for me and for himself. 'It was good of you to come on a Saturday night. Cigarette?' He pushed a heavy pile of papers from one side of the table to the other, lifted files, folders and books and eventually found a crushed packet of Players. The matches, a giant box, he found under the papers that covered a dresser with hideous carvings of cat-heads, presumably the piece of furniture he'd bought at Tiger's shop. I began to notice other signs of his mania, the framed drawings of cats on the walls, pictures of cats out of maga-

149

zines, china cats, pottery cats, and one really handsome cat carved in alabaster.

'I suppose you're finding all this rather odd,' he said, self-consciously. 'My ringing-up under another name –'

'My nurse was hoping you were a new client.'

'In a way I am.'

'Are we to have your records in the name of Archibald?'

'Yes, that would save – er – confusion. You see, I don't want my wife to know about this place; well, not just yet.'

'I saw your wife this evening.'

'Oh, how is she?' asked Topper, absent-mindedly. We might have been talking of a casual acquaintance he hadn't seen for months.

'She's worried about you.'

'About me?' He sounded genuinely surprised. 'But I was in Hampstead only – let me see – three days ago.'

'May I ask you a personal question? Do you intend leaving your wife?'

'*I*, leave Mary! Certainly not! Whatever gave you such an idea?'

'Well, I think your wife is expecting the worst. It's not altogether surprising.'

'Good heavens! I thought she had more sense.'

'Mr Topper, she's wondering where you're staying the nights you're not at home.'

'Here, of course.'

'She doesn't know that, does she?'

'Oh – er – I see. Poor little Mary. I suppose she's got a bee in her bonnet about another woman.'

'Is there one?'

'Good Lord! Of course there isn't.'

'How is *she* to know?'

Topper rubbed a hand over his eyes. There was no trace of madness or abstraction in them when he looked at me. 'I'm sorry, Morton; I'd better explain. You see I've been stuck in

150

a book I've been writing – been thinking of nothing else.'

'A book about cats?'

'Yes, of course. I've just finished correcting the proofs.'
He rummaged among his papers and brought out a large
volume, beautifully illustrated with drawings and paintings
of every imaginable kind of cat. 'It's been rather an exacting
job – I couldn't have done it with Mary and that poodle of
hers about the place – I'm afraid I've rather pushed the
problem of Mary out of my mind. But of course *something*
will have to be done now; if Mary saw the television programme –'

'You're appearing on television?'

'I'll have three programmes, on successive Sundays –
under the name of Archibald, of course.'

'You weren't expecting to keep *that* from your wife, were
you?'

'Well, I meant to tell her today. But I couldn't leave Sally
– and now there are the kittens. And I have a full day tomorrow.'

'On Sunday?'

'Yes, one of my biggest customers from Canada – Morton,
will you do something for me? I mean, treat it as a consultation or – well – special treatment. Will *you* tell Mary for me?
Perhaps be with her for the show. It'll be rather a shock to
her.'

'What do you expect me to do? Hold her hand?'

'More or less. Would you mind?'

I did mind. Mrs Topper should have had a psychiatrist
hold her hand, I thought. She'd spent a sleepless night in the
empty house, and she looked it. Naturally, Pooky too was
restless. Not being a psychiatrist I didn't know what was
better, to tell Mrs Topper her husband had written a book
which was on the way to best-sellerdom, or to let her ramble
on about their happy marital past. I decided on the latter,

chiefly because it was the line of least resistance.

'I was madly in love with him,' she told me, gathering up photographs of Topper as a baby on a bearskin rug, of Topper at school and Topper with his first motorbike. 'He was the breath of life to me. My father was dead against my marrying him – a fellow without a penny. You have no idea to what lengths I went to see him. And then, one night – in the middle of the night I got up, dressed myself, and went to his lodgings. I threw stones at his window until he heard me – I'll always remember that. It was terribly cold – the rain was pelting down. And the gutters were running – there was such a noise, I thought he'd never hear me. But he came down and let me in.'

Mrs Topper laughed. 'I don't know which of us was more scared – I kept thinking he was going to give me a baby – he never did,' she said sadly. 'And then, at breakfast-time, I walked in on my father and told him I'd spent the night with Archy. He didn't have much imagination – only in business – so, well, he agreed there was nothing he could do and I'd have to marry the boy – and now it's all over.'

'Of course it isn't,' I said.

But she wasn't listening to me. She was wrapped up in her misery. 'It wouldn't have done him any good if I'd gone on being a soft little thing. He needed a woman with a business head – someone he could discuss things with. He never was any good at making friends with other men; not the kind of friends on whom he could lean. And Archy needed to lean – there are two sides to me; I don't really like taking the initiative, but with a man like Archy I *had* to.'

I was listening to this miserable hard woman, and thinking of Julia. I was thinking of other couples where the husband had finally produced the kind of wife he did *not* like. I'd have to watch out. I did not want Julia to become a Mrs Topper drooling over an animal and treating me like an unwelcome hawker.

'You know,' Mrs Topper's face had softened. 'Archy is a very capable man. He's built up a business of his own from scratch, with very little capital. But it's always been I who gave him the ideas. He isn't an imaginative man – he's even a bit of a stick-in-the-mud.'

'That's where you misjudge him,' I said. 'If you –'

'Surely I know my own husband.' The sharpness and superciliousness had come back. 'I am the best judge of his character.'

I had been watching the French clock on the mantel-piece. It was almost time for Topper's show. 'Mrs Topper, if you switch on your television set you'll see your husband, and you'll discover that you *have* misjudged him. He's written a fascinating book – the first edition's been sold out before publication.'

I went and switched on the set myself; she was just sitting there, staring at me, her face changing expressions so rapidly that I began to fear I *would* have to pick up her ugly little paw, which would have been neither ethical nor enjoyable.

'Mr Archibald,' the Television Interviewer smiled at the invisible audience, 'I'm sure the viewers enjoyed your un-usual programme as much as I did. We'll look forward to seeing more of your delightful films and drawings at the same time *next Sunday*.' The picture faded on a stately puss licking her kittens.

Mrs Topper kept staring at the screen. 'Why didn't he tell me? Why did he have to do all this on his own? Surely he could – no, he couldn't. I can see that now,' she added, almost humbly.

The telephone rang. She shook herself, not unlike Pooky, came out of her daze, and went to answer the call. 'Don't go, Mr Morton,' she said, holding a hand over the receiver. 'It's my husband – yes, of course I'm listening. I'm all right Archib – darling. How are you? – Mind? – How wrong

153

you've been! It was marvellous, darling! – How nice of them! I? – You really want me to come? – Good – that's wonderful! – Mrs *Archibald* – no, I won't forget. Where is it? You're picking me up at home? – oh, thank you darling. There's nothing the matter with Pooky – all right, I'll be ready – Oh! Congratulations, darling!'

She put down the receiver and turned to me. When she smiled, showing a mouthful of fine teeth, one could almost see why Topper did not want to leave her. 'He's asked me to his TV party.' She pulled out the dirty Woolworth bag from behind a chair. 'Mr Morton, this was a consultation I won't argue about – worth every penny – how much?'

I was *not* going to branch out into the world of humans and psychiatry. 'Ten pounds,' I told her, keeping a straight face.

'Ten pounds?' Her hand hovered half in and half out of the bag. 'If I pay you cash I get ten per cent off, don't I?'

'No, Mrs Topper.'

'But that's normal business practice!'

'I'm not a business man.'

'Oh, well.' She kicked the bag back behind the chair. 'My husband can pay your bill.'

I supposed there *was* a chance Mr Archibald would settle this account.

When I got home Julia was sitting in the lounge with the windows wide open on the Mews, sewing 'little garments' like those she was wearing – the shortest red shorts and the kind of sun-top she appeared to keep up over her small bosom by faith and will-power.

I thought it hadn't been much of a summer for her, staying in a mahogany-furnished house that always had an air of winter about it, spending the few hot weeks in town helping me with the clerical work or Muriel with the cooking.

While the dogs crowded round greeting me I indulged in

a day-dream – of Uncle Simon signing a partnership agreement, of a winter honeymoon somewhere in the snow and
the sun. In Switzerland Julia would be able to go on wearing
those short shorts of hers. Yes, but until Simon had given me
a partnership in the practice it would be as well if he didn't
know that Julia disliked wearing things that covered her
thighs. In my opinion she looked entrancing in her winter-
wardrobe of furry boots, shorts or velvet vine-leaves and
jerseys, but Simon and our more conservative clients might
disagree with her style.

'How did it go, darling?' She looked up from her sewing,
dropped it on the floor and held out her arms to me.

'Mrs Topper – chastened – is going to her husband's TV
party.'

'I'm glad they're all right.'

I picked Julia up, sat down in the chair, and put her on my
lap. While I kissed her the snake, as usual, came up and
hissed at me.

'When are you going to stop Cobby's jealousy?'

Julia laughed. 'Don't you think it's sweet?'

'Not very.'

'Michael, it's rather marvellous – Cobby's only guarding
me.'

'Is she?' I pulled down her will-power top. She protested,
holding me tightly against her breasts. 'Michael, stop it! Do
you think I'm wearing this blouse for *your* benefit?'

'For our mutual benefit, darling – a blouse you call it?'

'Michael, stop! Muriel might come in.'

'It's Muriel's evening off.'

Julia wriggled out of my arms and pulled up her 'blouse'.
'She'll be back soon, Michael – do you know where she goes
in her free time?'

'She has a sister, hasn't she?'

'Yes, sometimes they go to a theatre together – but mostly
she visits people – old people who are lonely; Miss Shaw, for

155

instance. Darling, when we're married will you expect *me* to do that?'

'If you want to.'

'I think I shall want to.'

'Well, not with Cobby.'

'But that's just it! Cobby would be terribly good for old people – she'd amuse them, don't you see! I've often thought how useful Cobby will be for the practice.'

I grabbed Julia. 'You'll make a terrible vet's wife.' Cobby reared, swaying about from Julia's side to mine, hissing into our faces.

'Ah, is nice to be happy like this.' Alfred Donizetti had come in without either of us hearing him. 'Carlotta used to enjoy very much when we were bridegrooms,' he added wistfully. 'I do not like to disturb – but it's Pippo. Perhaps Pippo had too much sun for a little bird?'

'What's the matter?' asked Julia.

'He fell off the perch and then he lie on his back and shake.'

'I'll come over with you right away.'

'I do not like to disturb – but if Joanna –'

Joanna's thrush! Alfred did not have to explain how terrible it would be if anything happened to the bird. I fetched one or two drugs I might need, and followed him across the Mews.

Even Carlotta Donizetti was worried. Though Pippo was back on his perch I gathered from Carlotta's description that he'd suffered a bout of vertigo and a fit. The thrush was sitting there with its feathers ruffled, head sunk on its chest; every now and again it swayed as if about to topple down once more.

I told Carlotta the bird was to have oiled seed and raw, grated carrot, and mixed Potassium Iodide into its drinking water.

'Pippo will get well?' asked Donizetti, when his wife had left the room.

'I hope so. If he doesn't look brighter tomorrow I'll give him an anti-histamine. Did Joanna see him fall?'

'No – was good luck.'

'So it was. If she notices anything tell her Pippo has a cold.'

'In the warmth? – Yes is possible. Joanna had a cold in the summer once. It was because of the empty Number Seven; that house, it makes the wall damp.' Donizetti's swarthy face suddenly became keenly animated. 'I have the idea! Michael, you get married, you need the house! Is simple, yes?'

'No. We want to get married, but I can't afford a house, certainly not in Knightsbridge.'

Donizetti shrugged his shoulders. 'Maybe we won't have house here either,' he said dejectedly. 'Carlotta say I'm cruel; she visited divorce-lawyer.'

'Do *you* want a divorce, Alfred?'

'No, but I understand. Carlotta is born English. She had good education. Is not like me, selling *popone* – melon – in not nice streets in Naples.'

'Yes, yes, but look what you've done since. You are a manufacturer of society gloves. The *Queen* wears your gloves.'

His own favourite boast did not cheer him up. 'Yes, I have good business – but Carlotta, she does not like the things I like.'

'The beautiful furniture you bought her?'

'Is not important. She say is bad for me to like beer in the Crown, and the Italian friends I have and the lady customers what ring up, and the horse races.'

'Have you ever taken her to the races?'

'No, she does not like.'

'She can't know if she's never been.'

'Carlotta will not come – so, she does not speak with me

157

any more.'

'She spoke to you *tonight*.'

'Because of the bird. Carlotta is educated woman; she know if bird died it would be very terrible for Joanna.'

'You must make her understand it would be terrible for Joanna if there were a divorce. Joanna's very fond of you.'

Donizetti nodded. 'Maybe Carlotta know – but she is angry. I said I do not go to the races, but when she ring up the office the girl say I went to the horses. Carlotta say, is bad, gambling.'

'All right, I'll tell you what we'll do. There's the big race-meeting at Kempton Park in three weeks' time. The Queen might be there. I'll give you two tickets for the enclosure. You tell Carlotta she'll be sitting near the Queen.'

'Ah, yes, if Carlotta could sit near the Queen!'

CHAPTER TWELVE

I heard Muriel, in the hall, making-up Carlotta's mind for her. Carlotta, outraged, had told Muriel what an insensitive man her husband was – knowing perfectly well how she felt about gambling he actually expected her to accompany him to Kempton Park races this Saturday. He'd been so persistent that he'd driven her out of her own house. If that wasn't cruelty, what was? Trying to force her to go to Kempton Park on such a miserable cold day, and for what. Gambling!

'You don't have to bet, Carlotta,' said Muriel, mildly.

'*He* will though.'

'Well, you wouldn't know what it's like if you've never been to the races – but naturally you don't want to go. It's quite understandable; foreigners don't have the feeling for horses that we have.'

'I'm not a foreigner,' Carlotta objected. 'I was born in London.'

'Yes.' Muriel managed to convey some doubt. 'Then it's just possible you might see why the Queen's so keen on racing; perhaps not though. Well, there's no point in talking about it. You've made up your mind you aren't going.'

There was a silence, the kind I'd heard so often over at the Donizettis' house when the windows stood open to the Mews, the kind of silence that usually broke in a crescendo of angry voices.

This time it didn't. Carlotta heaved a sigh. 'Well, I don't know. Alfred says the Queen will be there. Muriel, what shall I wear?'

Some special instinct seems to tell my clients when I am about to leave London, and that is the moment they choose for presenting me with their more appalling animal problems.

That day the problem was Dr Armstrong's fox. Julia and I had just put our raincoats in the car when Peter Armstrong drove up. On the luggage rack, on the roof of his Jaguar, was a large blanket-covered box which turned out to be Renard in a stout wire cage.

Before I could prevent it Peter had hoisted the thing down, dived inside the car, and thrown a bottle of champagne into my arms.

'Elizabeth has had a son!' he announced. 'Eight pounds two and a quarter ounces! Come on you two, the champagne's iced, let's drink to our boy!'

We congratulated him and I said we'd be pleased to drink young Armstrong's health provided we could do so quickly. I told him I was looking after Miss Skeffington's horses and had to get to Kempton Park well before the race.

'Plenty of time,' he said, picking up the fox's cage.

'What's the matter with Renard?' I asked.

'He's quite all right except for the usual bit of tail-biting. But we can't keep him with a baby in the house. Well, you know him, Michael; he's quite gentle – just a bit mischievous. I did ring a few zoos, but none of them requires a fox just now.' Peter followed me indoors, heaving up fox and cage. 'Good God!' He stared at the peacefully coiled Cobby. 'A snake! What's it doing here.'

'I happen to be living with it,' I told him. 'A splendid wild creature – remember?'

'Oh well, that's jolly; then you won't mind the fox.'

'I would mind the fox. Do be reasonable, Peter. We have also –'

'I am being reasonable. If you're already living with a snake a mere fox won't make any difference.'

160

'But our dogs –'

'Only four,' he said, getting tangled in their welcome. Alsatian and poodle, spaniel and pug pushed past him and went to sniff at Renard in his cage.

'Peter, this isn't *my* house,' I pleaded.

'I know,' he said in his most soothing psychiatric-couch voice. 'But don't forget your uncle's a vet too. And anyway, he's abroad.'

'He may be back any day.'

'Then let me tell you, Simon used to be very good with Renard.'

'I'm sure he was, but that doesn't mean he'd like to live with the fox.'

'If he doesn't mind a snake he won't mind my fox.'

I wasn't sure whether Simon would appreciate either. 'Peter be a good chap and take your fox away. We have nowhere to keep him.'

'But I don't expect you to keep him. Just let him stay with you until you've found him another home.'

Peter's 'splendid wild' creature was having a hard time. The four dogs were storming the cage with a barrage of barking neither Muriel nor Julia could stop and Cobby – for once fully in agreement with our other animals – had crept on top of the cage and was trying to squeeze inside. The fox, pretending indifference, was biting his tail in a frenzy of 'nerves'.

There was only one thing we could do if we were to get to Kempton Park at all. I picked up fox and cage and put them in the surgery. Only then did Peter allow us to knock back the champagne and go.

Anxious as I was to examine Septimus and Cybele before the race the 'human element' seemed bent on obstructing me, on preventing my keeping a watch on Miss Skeffington's horses. Julia and I had got in sight of the stables when Tiger, his head deeply sunk into the collar of his sheepskin coat, blocked our way.

'Hello,' he said, disconsolately.

'Claire here?' I asked, hoping he'd let me pass.

'Yes, with the Hoopers and the Duke.'

'See you later.'

'Who wants to marry Claire?' he asked, a spurt of unexpected fierceness darkening the freckles in his pale, long face. 'Is it Winky?'

'Not that I know of.'

'Then who does know?' I had never seen Tiger in such a positive mood. 'It's most peculiar.'

I thought I might get away more quickly if I let Tiger get whatever was bothering him out of his system. 'What is?' I asked.

'Well, you know I'm going to the States with *Three Brassieres to Bond Street*. Claire – I thought it was understood – was to look after the shop altogether in future; I'm working on a new play. All of a sudden she tells me she's going to leave the shop as soon as I get back to England – said she might get married. I can't understand her at all.'

'Girls do get married,' said Julia.

'Yes, but Claire! Why didn't she tell me before? As a matter of fact she's been rather strange lately; there are things she just won't discuss with me any more.'

'Such as sound sex life?' I asked.

'I say!' Tiger's head shot out of his collar. 'That's jolly clever of you Michael.'

It seemed he'd driven Claire to taking my advice; I only hoped it had been good advice. I could never tell with intellectuals who wrote plays such as *Three Brassieres to Bond Street*. But Tiger did appear genuinely perturbed by this slight inconvenience in his personal relationship with Claire.

'Claire hasn't told you whom she wants to marry?' I asked.

'Not a thing.'

'It couldn't be you by any chance?'

'Me?' Tiger's ears reddened.

'Yes, why not,' said Julia.

'No, I shouldn't think so. Though I did wonder, if the play does well in New York – I mean, I'd have money.'

'Who cares about money!' Julia made it sound as if no one in their senses did.

'Well, not normally,' agreed Tiger. 'But Claire's people are frightfully wealthy.'

'They wouldn't object to Claire marrying you, would they?' I asked.

'I don't expect they would. But when a girl like Claire marries someone who hasn't got a bean people always get the wrong idea.'

'That's true; though you, of course, are in an exceptional position. You're the author of a successful play. Wealthy women quite often prefer to marry a famous rather than a wealthy man.'

Tiger nodded. 'Well yes; there was Inga Venderbolt who married that Welsh poet,' he said thoughtfully. 'And Florence Entwhistle –'

'Hi there!' Allerton Newtonson, dressed from head to foot in waterproof quilting, came and shook hands with us. 'What do you know, Tiger! Last night I showed that Chinese screen to Lord Billbrother, and you know what he said? In all his years out East he never saw a finer. *Some* shopping!'

'Are you going to do any more shopping?' I asked.

He gave his shrewd, friendly grin. 'Mr Morton, do *you* know what that Sidney Franks is asking for Miss Skeffington's horses?'

'Yes, he told me.'

'And you think it's a fair price?'

'That's not a fair question, Mr Newtonson.'

163

'Oh sure, sure. You needn't answer it. But I'm no sucker.'

'I know you aren't.'

'As regards horses,' he said, 'I follow my intuition. If Cybele and Septimus show some guts today – if they're placed at all – I'll buy them.'

'That's not exactly following your intuition,' I said.

'I mean, Mr Morton, if the colt and the filly are placed I'll buy the lot of them.'

I suddenly noticed that Julia had disappeared. Looking towards the stables I saw her at one of the doors signalling me with both arms.

'You'd pay Miss Skeffington's price?' I asked.

'Sure, sure.'

'You won't regret that bit of shopping either,' I told him, making off towards Julia who was urging me on.

I passed a bunch of stable-boys, apparently engaged in some private betting, and groups of trainers, jockeys and owners.

'Quick,' whispered Julia. 'I've just seen Miss Skeff give something to one of the horses – not hers.'

'Good God, no! Not Miss Skeff!'

'I tell you Michael, I saw her.'

I walked straight in, with Julia following me, and at that moment Miss Skeffington was putting her hand into her coat pocket.

'Miss Skeffington!'

She turned, smiling and unhurried. 'Ah, Mr Morton! And dear Miss Hanley. How very kind of you to come.'

It seemed preposterous that this sweet-faced innocent-looking old lady should be engaged in doping horses. It didn't make sense. 'Miss Skeffington,' I said. 'My fiancée believes she just saw you – er – feed one of the horses.'

'Oh yes, I've given that pretty little horse over there a lump of sugar. It looked so lonely.'

'You'd be in great trouble, Miss Skeffington, if anyone other than Julia had seen you do that. Don't you know it's against the rules to give anything at all to horses before a race?'

'The poor things. Mr Morton, you must be wrong, because dear Sidney just gave me the sugar.'

'For *after* the race.'

'No, no. He told me to see the horses now.'

I was getting hot under the collar. Someone was bound to come in at any moment. What was I to do? I knew I should report that lump of sugar, whether it was sugar or not, and I knew I couldn't do it without getting Miss Skeffington into frightful trouble. Who would believe that this daughter of a great horse owner didn't know the rules against feeding horses before a race? One had to know Miss Skeffington well to believe in her innocence.

I took her by the arm and led her outside, where no one could listen to us. 'I'm certain you misunderstood Sidney,' I told her. 'You mustn't mention this on any account, Miss Skeffington, or we'll all be in trouble.'

'Oh dear, how silly of me. I won't tell anyone, if you say so Mr Morton.'

'Now, would you give me the sugar please.'

She obediently produced a handful of lumps. 'I suppose dear Sidney expected me to know the rules. My dear father used to become quite annoyed with me because I took so little interest in racing. If Sidney hadn't persuaded me to keep the horses a little longer –'

'Yes, I understand. Miss Skeffington, where is Sidney? Do you know?'

'Sidney and Jake were going back to the horse-box. I think there's something wrong with the piece that connects the box with the car. Cybele had to travel in the trailer because –'

'Thank you, Miss Skeffington.' I thought we had no time

for irrelevant explanations. 'See you later.'

She watched us run off, with a puzzled frown on her face.

By a bit of luck Sidney was inside the box, collecting some horse-blankets. I told Julia to stay out of sight both of Jake, who was talking to his girl, and of the open doors of the box.

'Hello, Michael,' Sidney greeted me. 'So you made it.'

'I told you I would.' I stayed in the doorway. 'Today the horses *won't* be doped.'

He shot upright and glared at me. 'What the hell are you talking about?'

'I'm talking about those lumps of sugar you gave Miss Skeff.'

I saw it come – that vicious kick at my stomach, and I got my fist in first, into Sidney's face. 'One more move from you and that sugar goes straight to the police.'

Sidney stopped himself from chancing another kick. He stood, rubbing his jowl. I could see him work out another line. 'Well, what do you expect, making accusations like that! It's disgusting – this from my own vet! Blackmail, that's what it is!'

'It is blackmail, and I'm not your vet, but Miss Skeffington's. Now listen! I know you doped Septimus at Windsor. You fed him a tranquilliser –'

'Nothing of the sort!'

'Shut up, Sidney. That horse behaved as if he'd been trained for a comic act; it was Tranquiline 13B all right. Today you planned that not only Miss Skeff's horses but one or two others as well should behave in a peculiar manner – less suspicious that way.'

'You're off your rocker!'

'It's no use Sidney, I know what you're up to. You weren't sure you'd keep your job with Miss Skeff if she sold her horses, so you were going to see that she didn't.'

'Miss Skeff would want me to stay on whether we have horses or not.'

166

'But with the horses the money's better, isn't it? Horses doped to lose races can bring in quite an income. I'm just letting you know you're finished. And I'll tell you what's going to happen right now. I shall lock you and Jake and his girl in this box, and if you make a sound until the races are over you'll be arrested on the spot. Keep where you are!' I looked at my watch. 'If I'm not out of here in a minute someone's going to hand over those lumps of sugar to the police.'

'Why don't you?'

'Because I'm satisfied that Cybele and Septimus aren't doped. I want them to run. And I want Miss Skeff to have her chance of selling them.'

'What about afterwards?' Sidney's assurance had vanished. 'What are you going to do?'

'That I'll decide later – Jake!' I called. 'You're wanted. Bring Lizzie, will you!'

I let them both in and then jumped down out of the box. 'Sidney, you can explain to them why they've got to stay with you until after the races. And remember, no sound from any of you.'

There was no sound from them while I drew the heavy bolts across the doors.

The day was not so bad after all. The wind had dropped, the rain-loaded clouds had stopped chasing across the course, and while the Queen and her party took their seats the sun came out.

The Duke came out of the scrum besieging one of the bookies. 'Always did fancy that colt,' he said, as if he'd been a betting man all his life. 'Never take a vet's advice, eh?'

'You backed Septimus for a win.'

'I most certainly did.' He held out a great wad of pound notes. 'Pretty good, what! I grant you he didn't make much of a show at Windsor, but I knew that colt had it in him. Now Morton, where do we go from here? What do you

167

fancy for the last race?'

'No tips.'

'We know what that means,' said Lady Jane, joining us. 'Mr Morton's Septimus' vet *and* Cybele's. I think I'll back Cybele.'

'Right.' The Duke scrutinised my face. 'Any objections, Morton?'

'Sir, Cybele's a fine filly, but don't expect me to know the opposition.'

'Cybele's a fine filly,' said the Duke, returning to his bookie.

'Dick!' called Lady Jane. 'Over here! Come over, Dick! Berry's giving better odds.'

Back in the enclosure I saw Tiger and Claire, arm in arm, and the Donizettis talking as if Carlotta hadn't seen a divorce lawyer. When she wasn't being hard on Joanna or furious with poor Alfred she really was quite a handsome woman in her Mediterranean way.

'Interested?' I asked her, cautiously.

She smiled. 'Well, Michael, the way Alfred talked of racing it just gave me the wrong impression. Of course – not being English – he didn't mention the things that are really important about it.' She leaned closer, wafting over me a whiff of some exotic perfume. 'Have you noticed Her Majesty? She is wearing Alfred's latest model.'

'Is nice glove.' Alfred reverently picked up his wife's hand. 'Same as what Carlotta wears. Is called Donizetti's Super Society.'

Miss Skeffington shook hands with Allerton Newtonson and then gave his big paw an affectionate pat. 'I do hope dear Mr Newtonson you'll be very happy with them.'

'I know I shall be, ma'am,' he said, smiling broadly. 'I reckon Her Majesty the Queen hasn't got a finer lot of Arabs. It's their stamina I like.'

Carlotta Donizetti seemed highly interested. 'I didn't know the Queen had Arabs – for the heavy work, I suppose. Do you think they're better than English, Mr Newtonson?'

'Well, ma'am, it depends on what you want them to do, and – of course – from where you get them.'

'Mine come from Little's Domestic Employment Agency. So far they haven't sent me an Arab maid. Which country supplies the best in your opinion?'

Alfred Donizetti and Newtonson exchanged glances and successfully bit down their laughter. Newtonson looked away. 'I should try an Algerian, ma'am, if I were you.'

Alfred stifled a sound somewhere between a hoot and a hiccup. The arrival of the Duke's party saved his equilibrium; his Grace, eyes shining, made straight for Miss Skeffington.

'Great filly, Cybele,' he announced. 'Thought she'd bring off a double for you, Miss Skeffington.' He patted his breast pocket. 'She certainly did for me. Where'll she be running next?'

'I think in America.'

'I guess so,' said Allerton Newtonson. 'Miss Skeffington's just sold me her horses.'

'Congratulations!' Lady Jane kicked her brother's shin. 'Dick, it's just as well for you. Your beginner's luck wouldn't last.'

'Quite right, Jane. Know what I've made this season, Morton? Eight hundred pounds – enough to take Rainbow to the States. They tell me those dog-psychiatrists are jolly expensive – but I reckon there'll be enough for the two of us if I don't waste money on hotels. I might stay with our Ambassador. Oh, there you are Claire! You see! Cybele it was!'

Claire, her hand in Tiger's, smiled. 'We didn't bet – but I picked a winner. Tiger and I are engaged to be married.'

Julia kissed Claire. Lady Jane kissed Tiger. The whole lot

were kissing each other.

'That's great!' Allerton Newtonson had just kissed Miss Skeffington. 'How say you all go back with me to the Dorchester?'

Claire laughed. 'How say you all go back with me to my flat, for dinner?'

Tiger was silently counting heads; the Duke, Lady Jane, Miss Skeffington, Allerton Newtonson, the Donizettis, myself and Julia, and Molly Hooper who had drifted up to us, her nose in the *Times Literary Supplement*. 'Darling,' Tiger whispered to Claire, 'how many chops –'

'It's all right, darling,' said Claire. 'It's organised.'

While our party tried to sort out who could and who couldn't accept, Claire took me aside. 'Don't worry, Michael, it won't be chops and Coca-Cola. I got Fortnum and Mason's in to do the thing properly – I thought if I didn't get Tiger to the boil today I never would. Oh Lord!' she giggled, 'I don't know what I'd have done with all the food and the waiters if it *hadn't* come off.'

Carlotta held out a beautifully gloved hand to Claire. 'I hope you'll have a lovely party, Miss Brown-Claremont. I'm so sorry we can't join you, but our baby-sitter has to be taken home. Good-bye, Duke, good-bye . . .'

The Donizettis got into their Impala and the rest of us scattered towards our cars. Suddenly Miss Skeffington put her hand on my arm; there was a crestfallen, guilty look in her eyes. 'Oh dear! Mr Morton, I'm getting so absent-minded. I quite forgot dear Sidney!'

I too had forgotten the trio locked in the horse box.

'Do you know where he is?' she asked. 'I do believe I haven't seen him since before the first race. How very strange!'

'It's all right,' I assured her. 'Sidney's waiting for me. Do go on with Mr Newtonson. I'll tell Sidney.'

'Well,' Miss Skeffington hesitated. 'Perhaps I should go in

Sidney's car. I mustn't hurt his feelings.'

'I don't think Sidney will be going to London,' I told her.

'Of course, he'll be busy with the horses.'

'Sidney may well want to find another job now that you've sold the horses.'

Miss Skeffington nodded. 'Oh yes. I do so hope he finds more rewarding employment. I always did think he should have a position of greater scope.'

When I let Sidney, Jake and Lizzie out of their horse box, I suggested to them they should find employment of *different* scope, in fact any job provided it had no connection with horses.

'Well, where's the police?' Sidney sneered. 'I suppose you haven't the guts to call them in without first analysing the sugar. Maybe you made a mistake, eh?'

'I *know* there's no mistake, as you'll find out if ever you take another job even remotely to do with horses. And now you'd better behave as if nothing had happened. Get Septimus and Cybele home; you won't give them anything they shouldn't be having if you know what's good for you. When the horses have gone to America you'll give Miss Skeff notice, in the proper manner.'

'And no handcuffs?'

'No handcuffs – for Miss Skeff's sake. She's not to be involved in a racing scandal; and you'd better watch your step.'

CHAPTER THIRTEEN

Fortnum's had been brilliant in coping with Claire's flat, with the two lilac-coloured walls and the two in mustard and lilac stripes, the black ceiling and the paper pheasants. After Fortnum's had done the work I could see that there was only one way of eradicating the puritan atmosphere of the place – *gold*.

Fortnum's had constructed a tent of gold streamers over the ceiling, caging in those ghostly pheasants, they had put up a long buffet of golden roasts, small Italian gold-chairs, and they'd even provided gold chrysanthemums and a couple of gold satin cushions for the lilac cats. One of the waiters seemed to have been specially appointed for his hypnotic effect on cats; while he stood staring at them Chou-en-Lai and Mao-tse-Tung actually remained on the cushions, languorously elegant, presumably as arranged by Fortnum and Mason's.

We drank to Claire and Tiger, and to Miss Skeffington, and to Allerton Newtonson, and to the Duke; and to Molly, because the blackmailing of her mother had succeeded. Rustler *was* going to be in the Horse of the Year Show and Molly *was* going to university. The waiters listened to our voices and when the noise had reached a certain pitch they put up little gold tables and served the roast.

'On my ranch,' Allerton Newtonson told Miss Skeffington, 'we have barbecues for two or three hundred. We roast a whole ox and a lot of pigs on the spits – but you'll be seeing it yourself, ma'am. There'll be a special party when you come to stay with us.'

172

'How lovely.' Miss Skeffington tried to sound enthusiastic. 'I'm sure it'll be an experience – there are so many things I want to see in America, Mr Newtonson, especially that road of which one reads so much in our papers; Broadway, New York, isn't it?'

'Place I read about in *Dog*,' the Duke was telling Julia. 'A mental sanatorium for dogs. Only thing is, Masters isn't too happy about it. Believe he likes animals best when there's something wrong with them. Funny thing about Masters; never known him to care about a perfectly healthy dog or cat. Chap hates the idea of Grey Rainbow on the tracks like any other greyhound.'

'What's Masters going to do while you're abroad?' I asked.

'Time he retired,' said the Duke. 'Going to let him have the cottage. Be staying with the Hoopers when I go down to Hazelbridge. I'm giving up my flat in town. Rainbow'll be better in the country. Dare say once Rainbow's making a show on the tracks I'll be able to afford rooms at my club. When we get back you'll look after the dog again, won't you Morton?'

'Yes, of course. How long do you expect to be away, sir?'

'Three or four months. I understand that's roughly the time it takes to cure allergy in a dog.'

'I hope it is curable.'

'Well – must give the dog a chance.'

'You won't be upset if Rainbow can't be cured, Dick, will you?' asked Lady Lane. 'After all you've done pretty well at the races, and horses . . .'

'Jane!' The Duke glared at his sister. 'How often do I have to remind you; horses have been the downfall of the Alan-spring family.'

'You will be in New York, Duke, won't you?' asked Claire. 'Tiger and I are going to take an apartment; we'd like you to stay with us. Tiger, we must get him a ticket for your play.'

'Thank you, thank you.' The Duke looked somewhat alarmed. 'Seen the play though, remember? first night.'

'Yes, I know,' said Claire. 'But you mustn't miss it in New York; the production will be different, won't it, Tiger? It's really lucky that you'll be in America when the play's on.'

One of the waiters came in from the hall and went to speak to her.

'It's all right, Tiger,' she said. 'Michael, I thought one of the gossip-writers got wind of our party, but it's for you – telephone.'

'Mr Morton? – Michael – is it you?' There was an undertone of hysteria in Muriel's voice.

'Yes, Muriel, what's the matter?'

'Everything!' She sounded uncertain whether to laugh or cry. 'Mr Morton – Simon – your uncle's coming home.'

'When?'

'He's sent a wire,' said Muriel, shakily. 'It's not very clear – he may be here in a day or two.'

'Good. Better make an appointment with your hairdresser.'

'Yes – oh, Michael! Something awful's happened. Joanna's thrush has fallen off the perch again – I think Pippo's dying.'

'I'll come right away. Does Joanna know?'

'She'd gone to bed; so that's all right for the moment. But Alfred and Carlotta are frantic.'

'Be there in ten minutes,' I promised.

The Silver Ghost would have got us home in less than ten minutes if she hadn't once again guzzled more petrol than I'd believed possible. The corner of St George's Hospital seemed to be her *bête noire*. As we turned it, wedged between a bus and a lorry, she began to cough and the engine failed

174

to respond to the accelerator. But, to her honour, the smell of petrol remaining in her tank did carry us to within ten feet of the Royal Ouse Yacht Club.

While I parked her Julia stopped a taxi, which brought out the Royal Ouse porter.

'Can't park here, sir.'

'Can't park anywhere else,' I told him. 'I'm out of petrol.'

'Well, sir, the police will tow –'

'Will you ring a garage for me? Tell them to fill her up and,' I gave him one of Simon's cards, 'bring the car round to this address.'

'No, sir, I can't –'

'Here are the keys.'

'Sir, you're not a member of the Club. I'm afraid –'

'I'm the Duke of Alanspring's veterinary surgeon – Look, I'm in a hurry. We'd appreciate your help.'

'That's all right, sir. I'll see to the car. Don't you worry.'

By the time we got to the surgery Pippo was dead. Looking at the small body of the thrush, lying on its back, I did not think I could have saved it if I had been on the spot.

Pippo had sung for all of us in the Mews; Joanna was not going to be alone in missing his voice. But Joanna hadn't loved the thrush for its voice; the bird had been the sole living creature she had felt to be exclusively her own. I think the body of the little thrush made Carlotta as well as Alfred realise how much they had failed their child. But that would be no comfort to Joanna when she got up in the morning and found her bird gone.

'We must find her another thrush,' said Carlotta, almost in tears.

'Yes, yes!' Alfred put his arm round her waist. 'Is very clever; Carlotta is right, yes, Michael?'

'Yes, another thrush,' I agreed. 'But where are we going to

175

find one at this time of night?'

'In Battersea,' said Julia. 'Mr Lightbody's – remember, Michael?'

'Yes, of course, he lives behind his shop. But whether he'll have a thrush –'

'Please, Michael,' said Carlotta, 'we must try. Alfred, bring the car round.'

CHAPTER FOURTEEN

'Ray's book doesn't say,' Joanna announced.

Muriel and Julia, Joanna's parents and I went on drinking tea, avoiding one another's eyes. I wished Cobby or our dogs would create some diversion, but they stayed put in front of the fire. Apart from Pug's snoring all was silent, damnably so.

'Ray's book doesn't say,' Joanna frowned, 'you know – about a thrush going black.'

'But Pippo's a special thrush,' said Muriel.

'Ye-es.' Joanna was not altogether satisfied. 'That's what I said to Ray – and he said, maybe.'

The idea of being defeated at this stage was almost intolerable. We'd spent a terrible night in search of Pippo's stand-in. Mr Lightbody, unable to produce anything other than canaries and budgies, had taken us the best part of a hundred miles in our search for a thrush. And in the end we'd had to make do with a young blackbird.

'Pippo,' I said, firmly, 'is the most unusual, special bird I've ever seen, Joanna. Don't forget an animal doctor sees lots of birds. You see, Pippo was very ill on Saturday, after you went to bed, so I had to give him extra strong medicine –'

'Black medicine?' I saw Joanna's idea taking shape. Her eyes began to look less doubtful.

'Yes, it was a black medicine and a yellow pill.'

'Is that why Pippo's bill's gone yellow?'

'Of course.'

'That's all right,' she said, as if I'd been apologising for turning Pippo's bill yellow. 'But Uncle Michael, did Pippo lose his voice too? It's different now.'

'That's right, he did lose his voice.'

'Like me when I had 'flu?'

'Yes.'

'I 'xpect Pippo's medicine was nasty like the one I had. But he's all right now,' Joanna added, with confidence.

'All this and Simon too!' exclaimed Muriel, when the Donizettis had gone. 'Your uncle may be here any moment.'

'Don't flap,' I said. 'I looked up time-tables. Don't think he could make it until the day after tomorrow.'

'There's so much to be done!' Muriel smoothed her forehead, and then made a gallant effort at flap-control. 'First of all, Michael, there's the problem of your agreement with your uncle. I've been going through the books; do you realise you have *not* collected the six new clients you need to get your partnership?'

'You must be wrong!'

'Here's the list.' Muriel moved her chair over, and Julia came to stand behind us. 'Claire Brown-Claremont and cats, one,' Muriel counted. 'Lady Jane and horses, two. The Duke and his greyhound, three. I suppose he does count even if he goes to America for a few months. Mr Archibald and cats, four. I don't think it would be unfair if we *don't* tell Simon that Mr Archibald happens to be Mrs Topper's husband, do you? Well, that seems to be the lot. Four. Miss Skeffington's fallen out; she's sold her horses.'

'Thanks to Michael,' said Julia, hotly. 'Wouldn't his uncle count her in?'

'I don't think so,' said Muriel. 'He's apt to stick to the letter of an agreement. He's not mean; it's a matter of principle with him.'

'That's inhuman,' protested Julia.

'Clever people are a bit odd – most of them; Simon's very gentle with animals. He's really rather wonderful –'

'My snake's a patient of Michael's,' said Julia.

'I wonder.' Muriel shook her head. 'No, dear, Simon wouldn't accept you and Cobby if you're about to become members of the family.'

'But I'm moving over to the Donizettis'.'

'Only for a while.'

Julia smiled, somewhat uncertainly. 'Just to break Cobby and me gently to Uncle Simon?'

'Well, to break it gently that we've acquired a giant cobra,' I told her. 'Good God, Muriel! I nearly forgot – we've also acquired the Armstrongs' fox.'

'Good,' said Julia. 'I've got an idea – and don't say *oh, Lord*, Michael. Renard's your fifth new patient if we can find him a new owner.'

'Yes,' agreed Muriel. 'That would be quite fair provided the Armstrongs remain our clients.'

'They've got the cat now,' I reminded her. 'It's on record, isn't it?'

'Yes, of course. That's all right then *if* we can find someone to take the fox. Now, who'd want a fox?'

'Masters!' exclaimed Julia. 'Don't you remember what the Duke said last night? He said he thought Masters likes animals best when there's something wrong with them.'

'But Renard's quite healthy.'

'He bites his tail, Michael.'

'That's true – I suppose one *could* say he's highly strung.'

'Oh, Michael!' Julia reproached me. 'Surely you can put it more strongly. Go and phone Masters.'

'Yes, do,' said Muriel. 'There isn't much time.'

'Masters, you can't possibly set free a fox that's been brought up in London – as a pet. He'd be dead in no time; especially Renard, who's not like other foxes.'

'Isn't he, sir?' Master's voice sounded more interested.

179

'Renard's most unusual; more sensitive than ordinary foxes. You see, he's afflicted with a nervous habit. He bites his tail.' There was no need to mention the legs of chairs and stiletto heels; they were not the Armstrongs' reasons for getting rid of the fox.

'Can't the tail-biting be cured?' asked Masters, suspiciously.

'Only for short periods. I don't think anyone could stop it permanently.'

'Is that why his people want to get rid of him?' Masters sounded as if he'd be prepared to take the fox's part against any owner of such kidney.

'Well, I suppose Renard's tail-biting *is* irritating for them.'

'Sir, I'll take the fox,' said Masters, fiercely. 'It's not reasonable, is it sir? There are people – as crazy as they make them – and no one bothers so long as they don't go about murdering other people. But an animal! Oh, no. Anything out of the way-like in an animal and the owners don't want it any more. Or worse,' he added, 'they go traipsing across the world to have what's different about the animal put *ight*. It's not fair, sir, I say. An animal's entitled to being *different* same as people are.'

'You're right, Masters,' I said, gratefully. 'Just one thing – I have the fox with me; he needs a home right away.'

'I see, sir.' For an awful moment I thought Masters had changed his mind. 'Well, I think his Grace won't object to the fox in the flat for a few days. We can take him to Hazelbridge when we go down next Saturday – yes, sir, it'll be all right; until I move to the cottage myself I'm sure my sister-in-law will look after Renard.'

'Five new clients,' said Julia, for the umpteenth time. We had spent the whole of the previous evening searching the year's records without finding that sixth client I needed for completing my part of the agreement with Simon. There

180

were any number of casual animal owners whose cats I had 'doctored', whose dogs I'd stitched up after their fights, whose canaries' eyes I'd treated. Perhaps some of them would call me again, but none fitted Simon's definition o *new regularly attended client.*

In the morning only Muriel looked at all unruffled. She went off to have her hair done, after which she and Julia were to have lunch together. Julia had persuaded Muriel to buy a new dress and Muriel had persuaded Julia that she needed advice in choosing among the new styles which, in her opinion, had been created by men with a loathing for the female shape.

I spent an unhappy morning trying to manage the surgery on my own, keeping owners happy while treating their animals, operating while keeping the anaesthetic going with my elbow, sterilising instruments myself, filling in record cards. I thought if Uncle Simon was idiot enough not to realise at last how wonderful Muriel was he wouldn't make the kind of partner I liked.

I had a steak-pie and a half pint at the Crown, where the bar was drearily empty, and then visited the man with the tropical fish (which had taken to eating one another) and the television naturalist who kept tortoises under his bed and terrapins in his bath. The tortoises had suddenly developed a habit of plunging down the fire-escape.

By the time I got home I had just about convinced myself that I'd failed to qualify for a partnership with Simon, and that in any case Simon was not qualified for a partnership with me. The gamble had cost me a thousand or fifteen hundred pounds and a year knocked out of my career.

When I heard Julia and Muriel laughing in the breakfast-room I thought it was most unfeeling of them. In fact I began to wonder whether Muriel was as marvellous as I'd thought. I had been wrong in taking on this crazy job, so maybe I'd been wrong about Muriel and Julia and the lot.

181

'Michael, what's the matter with you?' asked Julia, as I walked in.

'Just a little attack of paranoia,' I told her, bitterly.

'Darling, don't be such a pig! Do look at Muriel!'

I looked. She was wearing a pretty dress of some white tweed with a neckline that plunged to stunning effect. Her hair, richly platinum was arranged in a young feathery style. 'Very nice,' I said.

'You're a brute, Michael,' Julia was quite angry. 'Just *look* at Muriel and say what you *really* think of the dress.'

I felt compunction. It was entirely my own fault if I'd made a mess of things. 'Perfect,' I said. 'I've never seen you look nicer, Muriel.'

'Rubbish!' She smiled self-consciously. 'But I'm happy. Here, Michael.' She handed me an envelope. It was a letter from Muriel's hairdresser, Monsieur Chevaleresque. Monsieur had written to say that he was the owner of five pekinese, three bitches and two dogs, that he wished to present the best of them at shows and especially Crufts, and that he would appreciate my taking charge of their health and general condition.

'New client number six,' said Julia, putting herself in my arms. 'Darling, isn't it wonderful?'

I thought it was, and that I was qualified after all for a partnership with Simon and that Simon was the best partner I could have and that Muriel was wonderful. 'How did you do it?' I asked her.

She looked somewhat guilty. 'Well, Michael, they really are nice little dogs.'

'Good enough for Crufts'?'

'I think so – if you can stop Madame Chevaleresque from overfeeding them. I didn't do anything unethical.'

'I see. It just happened to be the twelfth hour for those little dogs to acquire a vet and – quite by chance – my twelfth hour for acquiring the missing client.'

'It was providential – Chinchin developing a funny little cough while I was about to be put under the drier. Imagine, Michael! If that peke had started coughing a few minutes later I might not have heard it. Such noisy things, driers.'

CHAPTER FIFTEEN

The noise two civilised little women can make when they spring-clean a room must be heard to be believed. Throughout the following day Julia and Muriel were returning furniture in Simon's room to where it had been before Julia occupied it, they washed the paint-work, remade the bed and put up fresh curtains.

After lunch I had to drag down Julia's luggage. Her cases were extraordinarily heavy considering they contained chiefly short shorts, velvet vine-leaves and will-power blouses. The sight of Julia's suitcases stacked in the hall, ready to be taken across the Mews to the Donizettis' house, depressed me. Cobby seemed to feel the same. Having crawled round those cases and bags, hissing and spitting, she finally curled up on top of them, tucked her head out of sight, and pretended to be dead.

The cold drizzle outside, the muddy Mews cobbles, and the people hurrying past in dripping raincoats just about matched my mood. While I drove about the city calling on a boy with a sick pet rat, a woman whose canary had developed a fungus and a cat with diarrhoea I kept worrying about Julia. I blamed myself for having let things slide. If we'd set about finding a home of our own there would have been no separation now, at least not as long a separation as we were likely to suffer because we had lived from day to day.

I returned home to a crowded evening-surgery of wet clients and sad, shivering animals. Muriel was in the kitchen, baking the biscuits Uncle Simon liked to keep by his bedside;

Julia should have left but I had no time to take her luggage across the Mews.

'I'll help you in the surgery,' she said. 'I can go immediately after, can't I?'

'That's all right, darling, no hurry,' I said, unhappily aware of her uncertainty. It was a miserable business that she should no longer have the assurance of being needed and wanted. But what could *I* do? Until Simon was back I myself could not be sure that there was a place for me in the house and the practice.

I felt sorry I'd told Julia she would make a terrible vet's wife. It had been said in fun yet it was the kind of thing women, in their off-moments, took seriously. Julia would undoubtedly get into all kinds of scrapes, but in her few months with us she had learned a great deal about assisting in the surgery.

I watched her handle a cat, which had been run over, with expert gentleness, calm a woman worried about the eyes of her dog, and console a little boy who protested loudly because I had to relieve him for a few minutes of his white rabbit whose ear had been bitten by a grey rabbit.

'Finished?' I asked her, dabbing a bead of blood off the mended ear.

'Ray and Mr Lightbody are here.'

I sent off t he child with the rabbit and went into the waiting-room.

Mr Lightbody jumped to his feet. 'Can you see us now, sir? I've been telling Ray, he's silly worrying about Admiral having puppies. I have plenty of puppies in my shop – they all got themselves born and no harm done to their mums. Isn't that right, sir?'

Ray, white-faced and close to tears, picked up the basket beside him and gave it to me. 'It's hurting Admiral,' he said, keeping his eyes averted.

The minute butterfly bitch was moving restlessly and her

belly, distended out of all proportion, looked as if it were a thing apart from the rest of her body. A barely audible crying came through her half open mouth. I realised that it would be some time before she'd produce her pups.

'Ray, have you had tea?' I asked.

The boy shook his head.

'Mr Lightbody, why don't you two go and have tea somewhere? Leave Admiral with us; I hope the pups will be born by the time you come back.'

Julia glanced at me, and understood. 'There's a nice place in Brompton Road,' she said, omitting to mention a coffee-bar nearer to us. 'Go on, Michael. You take care of Admiral. *I'll* tell Mr Lightbody where it is.'

'Don't want any tea,' I heard Ray object as I was taking the little bitch into the surgery.

Julia had managed to tell Mr Lightbody to stay away as long as possible, but even so we had to expect them back in a couple of hours at the most. I doubted whether that would give us sufficient time for delivering Admiral. The tiny bitch had been seduced by a much larger dog and the three pups in her belly were too big for her delicate build.

For more than half an hour I manipulated Admiral's fragile body. Every now and again it looked as if the pups might begin to come out in the normal way, and every time her strength ebbed and I was back where I'd started.

'It won't do,' I told Julia.

'Instruments?'

'Only thing.' I decided even if I did succeed in delivering the pups normally there was too much danger of serious damage to the mother.

'Quite right, Michael,' said a voice beside me. 'It'll have to be a caesarian. That's what *I* would do.'

'Anaesthetic ready, Julia?' I asked. Suddenly it occurred to me that the voice approving my decision had been a

186

man's voice. I looked up but there was only Julia, staring at the door to the hall. 'What was that?' I asked, taking my hands off Admiral.

'I don't know.' Julia looked vague and rather worried. 'He just walked in.'

'Uncle Simon!' It dawned on me I'd seen a flash of apple-green – Simon's Lillywhite's anorak. 'Take care of Admiral!' I shouted, dashing out.

He did not even notice me. He was on his knees in the hall, in front of Julia's luggage, stroking the sulky cobra, trying to coax her head from beneath the tightly coiled body.

'You're back then,' I said, inanely.

He looked up, giving me an ecstatic smile. 'It's a grand surprise, Michael – really clever of you! Whatever I expected I didn't think you'd have a thoughtful idea like this – where did you manage to get the cobra? A very fine one it is too.' Cobby had at last consented to being seen and was swaying her head from side to side like a primadonna. 'As good as any snake I saw in India,' said Uncle Simon. 'That's where it occurred to me that we English are hopelessly stodgy in our choice of pets. It's odd, isn't it, that we don't go in for snakes. I've been thinking of importing a few.'

'Mr Morton!' Muriel appeared, wearing her new dress. She must have accomplished the fastest quick-change act ever.

'Mrs Whiting!' Simon jumped to his feet and impulsively embraced her. 'Muriel!' He kissed her, emerging after a while with a completely stunned expression on his face. 'Weird – you were the only thing I missed while I was abroad.'

'Muriel, a *thing*?' I asked.

He looked at me, taken aback. 'Well – no. You've no idea how good it is to see women again whose bodies are covered up.'

187

I suppose the expression on my face told him what I thought of his appreciation of women. He grinned at me. 'Oh, go to hell, Michael! – Muriel, it's fine to be home.' This time it was Muriel who kissed him.

It made Cobby furious. She reared up and hissed, and when that didn't alarm anyone she puffed up her head as big as it would go.

'That's interesting,' said Simon, regarding the angry snake. 'Very interesting, this jealousy in animals. I didn't know that snakes responded similarly to – poodles for instance. Yes – a clear case of jealousy, don't you think, Michael? By the way, what's the luggage the snake's been guarding. Anyone staying with us?'

'The girl you saw in the surgery – don't worry, she's leaving today,' I told him.

'The owner of Cobby – the snake,' said Muriel.

Simon's face fell. 'No! *Must* she go?'

'Perhaps not,' said Muriel.

'You tell the girl,' Simon said in his clear I'm-in-charge voice. 'What's her name?'

'Julia Hanley.'

'You tell young Julia I'd consider it bad manners if she left the moment I return. Right, that's settled. Mrs Whiting – Muriel – what have you done to your hair?'

'It's different,' I said, 'and I suppose you don't like it.' I was prepared to defend both Muriel and myself against old Simon's mahogany-mindedness.

'You're an ass, Mike! Muriel's hair is terrific – funny, first time I've noticed that. Yes, my dear, very pretty.'

'Rubbish!' Muriel blushed with embarrassment. 'This is perfectly ridiculous – what on earth are we doing, standing about in the hall!'

'I want a hot bath,' said Simon. 'Yes, Michael, what are you doing, standing about in the hall? Get on with your work. You don't expect *me* to deliver that bitch, do you?'

I was in the middle of lifting the second live puppy out of Admiral's thin-walled belly, when Muriel and Simon walked into the surgery. He looked a pretty good fifty – lean, weather-beaten, virile. Muriel had put a moss-green velvet coat over her white dress, and she was wearing the highest stiletto-heels I'd ever seen.

'Neat,' said Simon, leaving some doubt whether he was referring to the incision I'd made in Admiral's belly or to Julia's white-coated figure. 'Miss Hanley, I've taken your luggage upstairs. You're staying.'

'Thank you, Mr Morton.'

He looked over my shoulder. 'Third pup alive? Poor bitch – it's been a bit much for her. Michael, you won't need the car tonight, will you?'

'Not unless there's an emergency.'

'If you get a call you can take a taxi.'

'A taxi?'

'Yes, Michael, a taxi. I take it you've hired one before now?'

'Don't think I've ever hired a taxi at the expense of the practice.'

'Bit mean of you.' He appeared to have no recollection of his past objection to taxi-fares. 'I'll have to buy you another car – unless you want to keep the Silver Ghost.'

'No thanks, not the Silver Ghost.'

'We'll see.' It sounded as if he'd already made up his mind to saddle me with that voracious masterpiece of a car. 'All right, carry on Michael. We're going out for dinner. If here's one thing I missed on safari it was a roast of sirloin, the way they serve it at Simpson's.'

'Did you miss sirloin as much as you missed Muriel?' I asked.

'That – you delinquent – is something I'll work out with Muriel over dinner. Good night,' at the door he turned, 'partner – damn it, you'll *lose* that bitch yet if you don't watch out.'

I had done the repair work on her belly, and we'd done all we could to resuscitate the butterfly bitch, but her heart still sounded faint and erratic. She lay on the operating table beside her pups, a little bundle of golden-brown fur limp with exhaustion.

'Michael, she isn't going to die?' Julia was too upset to mop up the tears that were streaming down her cheeks.

'I wish I knew.'

The sound of the door-bell made her jump. 'They're back – what am I to do with Ray?'

'Just keep talking.'

She returned a moment later with Alfred Donizetti. 'Ray and Mr Lightbody are with Joanna. Carlotta's given them tea.'

'Good, Alfred, can you keep them there?'

Alfred came and examined the inert bundle on the table. Apart from the wing-ears it looked smaller, more vulnerable than ever. 'Is sick dog,' he said. 'But is all right for a little bit. Carlotta promise Joanna can have one of the puppies. Is good, Carlotta, eh? The children find names for the new dog – is busy Ray and Joanna. Carlotta say the uncle is home again, he look healthy and –'

Alfred's chatter became unbearable. I could hardly hear Admiral's heart. The children were occupied for a while, so far so good, but what if Admiral died?

Alfred had got on to the subject of Carlotta being an educated woman, being good about something or other, being pleased with him over something or other. That at any rate was new. 'Carlotta agree with me,' he told us. 'What made all the trouble was the empty Number Seven. Is good idea, yes, Michael?'

'What?' I asked, exasperated.

'What! My buying empty Number Seven. You listen! You get married and you rent the house from me. When you have money you buy Number Seven for same price, eh?'

'You're a darling,' said Julia, gazing at Admiral.

Alfred didn't seem to notice her joylessness. He beamed at us. 'It was Carlotta – she say you been big darlings when Joanna's bird drop dead.'

Yes, we'd be able to afford that house, I thought without satisfaction, looking at Julia's tear-stained face.

'Michael!' she exclaimed, 'Michael, look!'

The three of us instinctively turned to the operating table. Admirals's eyes were wide open, the butterfly ears quivered, she sniffed at her squirming offspring, and slowly sat up. Languorously her small pointed muzzle touched one puppy and another and then, with a sudden spurt of will and purpose, she began to lick and groom them.

'Oh, Michael!' Julia and I fell into each other's arms, across the operating table. 'We *can* afford it! The house is all right! Admiral's all right! Everything!'

There was, between us, the sound of Admiral's tongue belabouring her puppies.

Julia's lips tasted of violets and salt.

STAR BOOKS

are available through all good booksellers but, where difficulty is encountered, titles can usually be obtained *by post* from:

Star Book Service,
G.P.O. Box 29,
Douglas,
Isle of Man,
British Isles.

Please send retail price plus 8p per copy.

Customers outside the British Isles should include 10p post/packing per copy.

Book prices are subject to alteration without notice.